# World Super-Powers

## David Church

## Nelson General Studies

Thomas Nelson and Sons Ltd.
Lincoln Way Windmill Road Sunbury-on-Thames
Middlesex TW16 7HP
P.O. Box 73146 Nairobi Kenya
P.O. Box 943 95 Church Street
Kingston Jamaica
308-312 Lockhart Road
Golden Coronation Building
2nd Floor Blk A Hong Kong
116-D JTC Factory Building
Lorong 3 Geylang Square Singapore 14

Thomas Nelson Australia Pty Ltd
19-39 Jeffcott Street West Melbourne Victoria 3003

Thomas Nelson and Sons (Canada) Ltd.
81 Curlew Drive Don Mills Ontario

Thomas Nelson (Nigeria) Ltd.
8 Ilupeju Bypass PMB 21303 Ikeja Lagos

© David Church 1978
First published in 1978
Reprinted 1979

ISBN 0 17 448107 1

Designed and illustrated by Hedgehog Design
Cover design by Eleanor Gamper

Filmset by Tradespools Ltd., Frome, Somerset
Printed in Hong Kong

# Contents

Forum of the super-powers: the United Nations
Security Council in session (*right*)

# Enter the super-powers

## Twin giants of the post-war world

In the Spring of 1945, the mighty armies of the USSR and USA were driving deep into the heart of Nazi Germany. On 25th April, Russian and American troops met on the banks of the Elbe, south of Berlin. Twelve days later, after the Russians had smashed their way into the centre of Berlin itself, the destruction of the Third Reich, which Hitler had boasted would last for a thousand years, was complete.

The war in the Pacific went on for another four months. But early in August American B29 Superfortresses, with the innocent-sounding names of Enola Gay and Bockscar, dropped atomic bombs on Hiroshima and Nagasaki in Japan. Gigantic fireballs 'brighter than a thousand suns', reduced the centres of both cities to ashes, killed over 100,000 people instantly and left another 300,000, some still unborn, to die painful and lingering deaths. Japan was forced to surrender.

The Second World War which had cost 30 million lives was over at last. Now America and Russia occupied the centre of the world stage over which loomed the mushroom-shaped shadow of the atomic bomb.

Of the chief protagonists in World War II who could have claimed to be leading world powers in 1939 Germany, Japan, Italy and France had all been defeated while Britain was exhausted by her efforts. But the Soviet Union had emerged from the war stronger than ever before. For, although ten million Russians had been killed, and thousands of Russian homes and factories had been destroyed, Russian forces now occupied the whole of Eastern Europe, and the Soviet government was ready to consolidate this position.

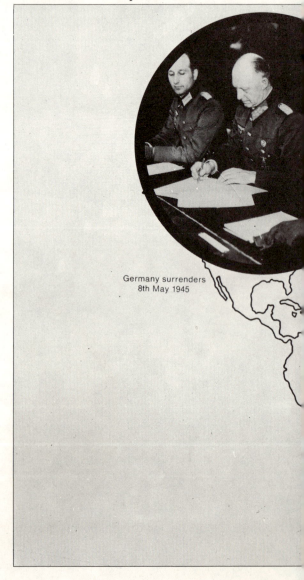

Germany surrenders
8th May 1945

No part of mainland America had suffered an air raid, only one out of every ten Americans had ever heard a gun fired in anger, America had the atomic bomb. In 1945 the USA was perhaps at the peak of its industrial and military strength relative to the rest of the world.

Over a hundred years earlier, the Frenchman Tocqueville had written that the USA and USSR seemed 'to be marked out by the will of heaven to sway the destinies of half the globe'. Since 1945, world affairs have indeed been largely dominated by the rivalry between these two nations. Not even Britain in the nineteenth century, secure in the possession of her empire on which the sun never set, had wielded such enormous influence over the rest of the world. Certainly no other country has ever before possessed the capacity to exterminate the human race as both the USA and USSR do today.

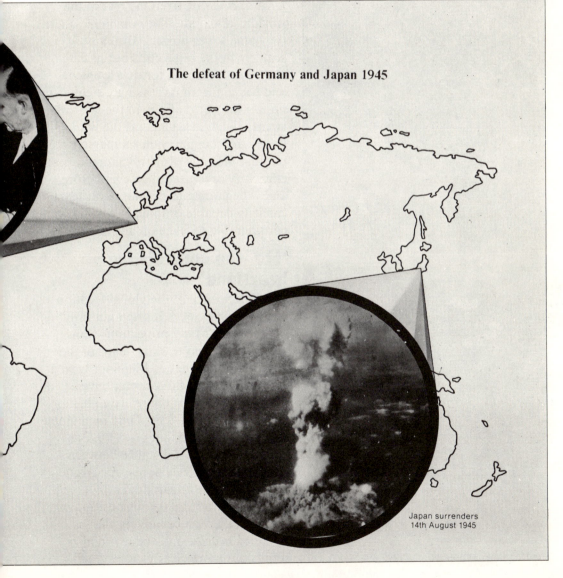

**The defeat of Germany and Japan 1945**

Japan surrenders
14th August 1945

## How super are the super-powers?

You may disagree with the criteria used opposite to evaluate the strength of the leading powers in the world. Perhaps you think that some factors should be weighted more heavily than others, that some indeed should be ignored completely. It could be argued for instance either that military might is, in the last resort, the only thing that really matters or that it should be discounted altogether in view of the nuclear stalemate. How do you measure military might anyhow?

Whatever criteria are selected, however, whatever league table is constructed, the huge gap separating the USA and USSR from the rest of the world is apparent. They obviously merit the name super-powers. China is scarcely in the same class but has enormous potential for development and has made an increasingly significant impact on world affairs in the last twenty-five years. China is the world's third largest country, has a massive population, now probably more efficiently organized than ever before, and is beginning to develop a nuclear capacity capable of inflicting considerable damage on any enemy.

## 'He who controls the heartland'

The significance of the global location of the super-powers is often not fully appreciated. Many projections commonly employed to show maps of the world, notably that of Mercator used at the beginning of this chapter, give a false impression of the relative positions of the USA and USSR. Only on a globe or world map like that on p. 10, does the relatively short distance between Russia and America across the Arctic ice cap become apparent. The strategically advantageous position of the Soviet Union occupying the so-called *heartland* of the world also stands out more clearly.

The Nagasaki atomic bomb, 1945

# The strength of the super-powers

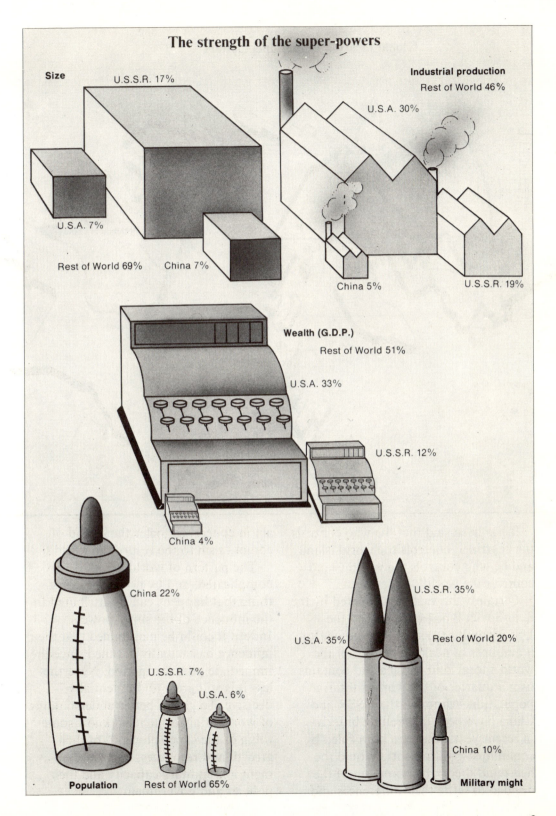

**Size**

U.S.S.R. 17%

U.S.A. 7%

Rest of World 69%　China 7%

**Industrial production**

Rest of World 46%

U.S.A. 30%

China 5%　U.S.S.R. 19%

**Wealth (G.D.P.)**

Rest of World 51%

U.S.A. 33%

U.S.S.R. 12%

China 4%

China 22%

U.S.S.R. 7%

U.S.A. 6%

**Population**　Rest of World 65%

U.S.S.R. 35%

U.S.A. 35%　Rest of World 20%

China 10%

**Military might**

9

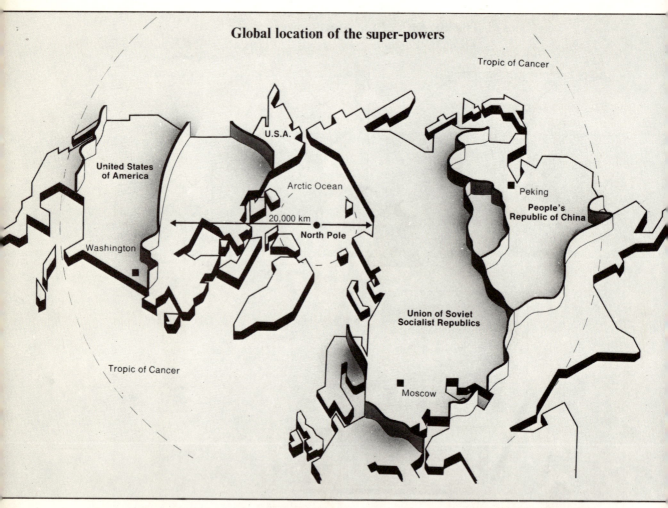

**Global location of the super-powers**

It has been said that 'he who controls the heartland controls the world island and he who controls the world island controls the world'.

Certainly the vast area covered by the Sino-Soviet bloc (ie China and the USSR combined) should be noted, for it amounts to nearly a quarter of the world's total land surface and contains over a quarter of the world's total population. Although the USSR and China have been quarrelling bitterly in recent years, they are both ruled by communist governments. Would the heartland theory be borne out, if they decided to settle their differences and act in concert to foster the spread of communism to the rest of the world?

The pattern of world affairs is very complicated, and by no means everything that happens can be attributed to the influence of the super-powers. Indeed it could be maintained that their influence has actually declined since the immediate post-war period. Nevertheless it is still great and potentially decisive. To gain a better understanding of world affairs, one must know something of the super-powers – of their growth and resources, their development and military capacity and their policies and government.

## Further reading and reference

*History of the Second World War*
B H Liddell Hart · Pan

*Recent History Atlas 1860 to 1960*
M Gilbert · Weidenfeld and Nicolson

*Geography of World Affairs*
J P Cole · Penguin

## For reflection

*'Nobody wants to remember Hiroshima; everyone needs to remember it.'* What do you think is the precise meaning of this statement? Do you agree with it?

The spot where the Hiroshima atomic bomb fell, 1945

## Analysis

**1**  On a world map, show the area occupied by the Third Reich and the Japanese Empire at their greatest extent in World War II. How close do you think these two powers came to securing world domination? Could they ever have gained control of the 'heartland'?

**2**  What was the significance of the meeting of Russian and American troops on the banks of the Elbe in April 1945?

**3**  Why did the Soviet Union suffer such heavy losses in World War II?

**4**  Which parts of the USA actually did suffer air raids in World War II?

**5**  Make a list of those countries which have occupied dominating positions in world affairs between the sixteenth and twentieth centuries. How did each one come to attain such a position, and why did each decline in greatness? Can you discern any pattern in the rise and fall of the various powers? How were the super-powers of previous centuries different from the super-powers of today?

**6**  What is Mercator's projection? What are its disadvantages? Why is it so commonly used?

## Discussion

**1**  An act of moral courage or an indefensible moral outrage.
What is your view of the dropping of atomic bombs on Japan?

**2**  Tocqueville made his prophecy in 1835. What do you think he based it on? What other nations or group of nations do you think might emerge before the end of the twentieth century to challenge the supremacy of today's super-powers?

**3**  The theory of the heartland was put forward at the beginning of the twentieth century. Do you think that it has any validity today?

**4**  Do you think that the influence of the super-powers in world affairs has declined in recent years? What evidence would you cite to support your views?

# Expansion and empire

## Size and scale

To appreciate the immense size of the super-powers, think of the longest journey you have made in Britain. Mark it on the map of the British Isles shown in the inset below, so that you can see its length against the background of the huge distances experienced in the USA and USSR. Between them the three super-powers occupy almost one third of the entire land surface of the earth, the Soviet Union alone covering about a sixth.

Although the possession of such vast territory makes communications difficult, it ensures that each state contains a wide variety of natural resources. In each country, however, there are also extensive tracts of mountain and desert which are of limited use for settlement and farming.

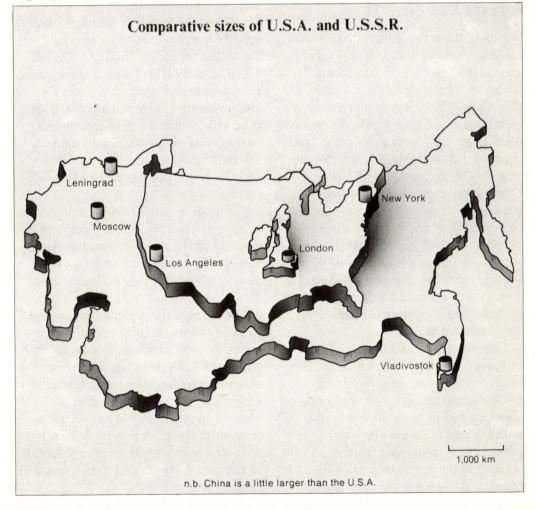

**Comparative sizes of U.S.A. and U.S.S.R.**

Leningrad

Moscow

Los Angeles

London

New York

Vladivostok

1,000 km

n.b. China is a little larger than the U.S.A.

Pasture and intensively-farmed agricultural land in China

## Mountains and plains, forests and deserts

Which of these two contrasted Chinese landscapes most closely accords with your mental picture of the country? It is probably the flat, fertile flood plain planted with rice. But in fact the greater part of China is actually made up of rugged, mountainous terrain like the cold, inhospitable Tibetan Plateau, 'the roof of the world'. The fact that China supports such an enormous population on such a relatively limited amount of lowland is rarely appreciated. Moreover, much of the north-western part of the country is composed of the Gobi Desert, the arid heart of Asia, which is cut off from rain-bearing winds by encircling mountains and sheer distance from the sea.

The mountains and deserts of interior China stretch across the southern border of her giant neighbour, the USSR. Lack of rain in the south renders about an eighth of the Soviet Union unfit for cultivation, while a short growing season seriously restricts farming in the northern part of the country. A glance at the map shows that the USSR extends into far more northerly latitudes than China or the USA, both of which lie mainly in the world's temperate zone. About half the total area of the Soviet Union lies north of 60°N where long, cold winters, perma-frost and poor soils make crop-growing almost impossible. This is an area of marshy pine forests and vast treeless plains (*taiga* and *tundra*), where the rivers freeze over in winter, and the Arctic coast is blocked by ice.

Although it is the smallest of the three super-powers, the USA can perhaps claim to be the most favoured physically. The Rocky Mountains and, to a more limited extent, the Appalachians are difficult areas to develop. So too is the desert in the south-west, most familiar to us as the spectacular backcloth for countless western films. But on the whole the USA does not suffer from the climatic extremes which characterize China and the USSR, nor does it contain so much hostile terrain. Consequently, the USA possesses a cultivable area only slightly smaller than that of the Soviet Union and almost twice as large as that of China.

# Birth of the super-powers

The super-powers have grown to their present sizes from modest beginnings. Each has expanded from a small area termed the *nuclear region*, the locations of which are shown on the map on p. 16. Some people would claim that each of these areas possessed certain geographical advantages, which made them pre-destined to form the embryos of great and powerful states. It is an interesting theory. Perhaps you think that the course of history cannot be determined in this way. Still it is worth checking to discover whether in fact these nuclear regions were especially favourable for farming and settlement and at the same time easy to defend against invaders.

The birth of each super-power was a painful process involving the organization and unification of the nuclear region.

In China this was accomplished as early as 221 BC by the Ch'in Emperor, whose cruelty and tyranny according to one writer anticipated that of Adolf Hitler by more than 2,000 years. Over a million men, for instance, many of them prisoners of war, are reputed to have died building the Great Wall, behind which the Chinese Empire developed, cut off by vast expanses of mountain, desert and ocean from other civilizations in Europe, India and Central America.

The rulers of Muscovy, nucleus of modern Russia, displayed equal ruthlessness, none more so than Ivan the Terrible, a contemporary of Queen Elizabeth I of England. Ivan has been compared to Stalin. Both certainly spent the last part of their lives immured in the Kremlin, from where they instigated hideous reigns of terror to sweep the

The Great Wall near Peking

country clear of all opponents, real and imagined. But both did much to increase the strength of Russia. By destroying the power of the nobles (*boyars*), Ivan consolidated the position of Muscovy as a national state while he also initiated the conquest of Siberia.

At an early stage therefore a highly centralized and autocratic form of government emerged in both China and Russia. Such a development was

Ivan the Terrible (1547–84)

# The growth of the super-powers

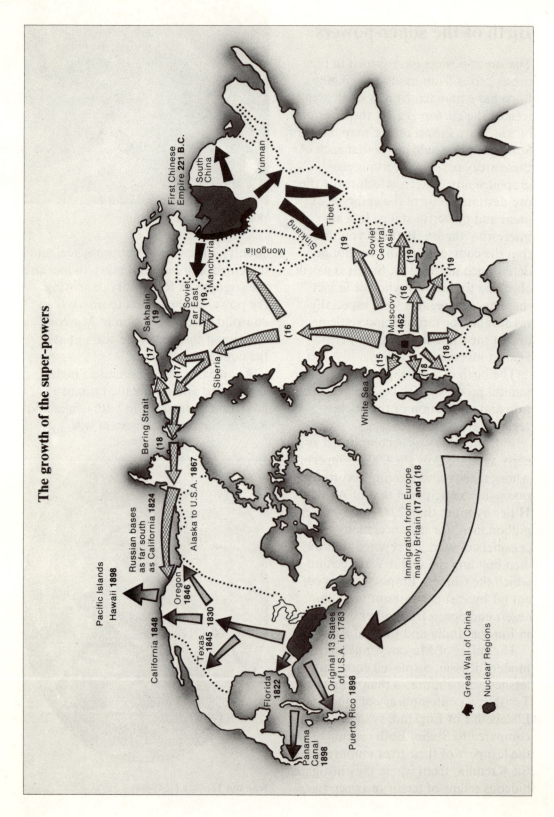

First Chinese Empire **221 B.C.**

South China

Yunnan

Tibet

Sinkiang

Mongolia

Soviet Central Asia

**(19**

**(19**

**(19**

**(16**

Muscovy **1462**

**(15**

**(18**

White Sea

**(16**

Siberia

**(17**

**(17**

Manchuria

Soviet Far East **(19**

Sakhalin **(19**

Bering Strait **(18**

Alaska to U.S.A. **1867**

Russian bases as far south as California **1824**

Oregon **1846**

California **1848**

Texas **1845**

Florida **1822**

Original 13 States of U.S.A. in 1783

Panama Canal **1898**

Puerto Rico **1898**

Pacific Islands Hawaii **1898**

Immigration from Europe mainly Britain **(17 and (18**

Great Wall of China

Nuclear Regions

probably inevitable, if both were to be efficiently defended against the enemies that pressed all about them, particularly the savage hordes that periodically came riding out of the steppes.

But the majority of the colonists who struggled to establish their settlements on the Atlantic seaboard of North America in the seventeenth and eighteenth centuries had left their European homelands precisely in order to avoid such repressive dictatorships. Many were refugees, like the Pilgrim Fathers fleeing from religious or political persecution; others were attracted by the prospect of staking out and farming their own land. All had come to America to seek wealth and liberty. Only when they felt that these were being threatened by British rule, did the thirteen English colonies join together to fight the American War of Independence (1776–83). When they had gained their freedom, it was still with some reluctance that the new sovereign states agreed to accept a limited degree of central authority in the form of a federal government and so establish themselves as the United States of America.

# The outward urge

Each super-power expanded from its nuclear region in the manner indicated on the map.

For China, expansion was a slow process involving the subjugation of warlike barbarian groups in the north and west and the gradual assimilation of people almost indistinguishable from the Chinese themselves in the south.

The Americans regarded expansion as their *manifest destiny* to create a vast

American pioneers reach the Rockies

continental state stretching from the Atlantic to the Pacific. They pursued this destiny so vigorously through conquest, purchase and treaty, that by 1853 the dream had become reality and, only 70 years after winning its independence, the USA had virtually assumed its present form.

The Russians were also motivated by a specific aim. Note how Russia's nuclear region was different from those of America and China. Behind Russia's outward urge was the desire to gain access to the open sea. You can trace the lines of the Russian drive to the Baltic and Black Sea on the map. Can you explain, however, why these exits were so superior to the White Sea and why it took the Russians so much longer to reach them than the Pacific coast, which is thousands of kilometres further away from Moscow? It is interesting to speculate on how far Russian foreign policy is still influenced by the age-long impulsion towards the sea. Can the rapid build up of Russian naval strength, her interest in the Suez Canal and her increasing activity in the Indian Ocean all be seen in this light?
*'One of the greatest feats of conquest in human history.'*
The Russian occupation of Siberia, which began in 1558 in the reign of Ivan the Terrible and was completed just over a hundred years later, was indeed an epic achievement, fit to rank alongside those of the Portuguese navigators and Spanish conquistadors which immediately preceeded it. Unnoticed by the world, the Russian advance to the Pacific was to have far-reaching consequences. In its wake, Russians even crossed the Bering Strait into North America to annex Alaska and establish bases as far south as California. More

significantly, the conquest of Siberia brought the Russians into contact with the Chinese. In the nineteenth century the Russians abandoned their American outposts, selling Alaska to the USA in 1867 for a mere 7 million dollars, but they occupied large areas in Central Asia and the Far East, which were formerly part of the Chinese Empire. Today these border lands are a cause for serious dispute between China and the Soviet Union.

## Minorities in China and the Soviet Union

It is as inaccurate to describe all the inhabitants of the Soviet Union as Russians as it would be to class all the people of the United Kingdom as English – imagine the outcry from the Scots, Irish and Welsh! For in the course of their expansion, both the Russians and Chinese absorbed various smaller national groups within the boundaries of their empires. There are no less than 91 of these groups in the USSR, each with its own customs and language. Most are very small, but there are also some significant minorities such as the Ukranians. In China minority groups form only 6 per cent of the total population, but they occupy nearly half the total area of the country.

The Russians and Chinese have granted a certain amount of self-government to their minority groups. In the USSR the area occupied by each major nationality has been formed into a republic as shown on the map. The different nationalities are not confined to their own republic; for instance all the republics include some Russians. Each republic elects its own government and also sends representatives to the central government in Moscow. In theory each has the right to leave the Soviet Union if it wants. Smaller nationalities within the republics, mainly within that of Russia itself in fact, live in smaller self-governing regions. Similarly the Chinese have set up semi-independent units of varying sizes for their national minorities, the largest being the five autonomous regions indicated.

The practical independence of all these self-governing regions is extremely limited, however. They are forced to accept the social and economic policies of the Communist Party, as carried out by the central government. Moreover, so many Russians and Chinese have been encouraged to migrate to the minority areas that the original nationality now often finds itself outnumbered in its own homeland. Although native languages are respected, Russian and Chinese are widely taught, and fluency in them is essential for advancement.

There is no official discrimination against racial or national minorities in the USSR or China but, from time to time, unofficial vendettas seem to have been mounted against Jews in the Soviet Union. Apart from Ukranians in the USSR, it also appears to be as difficult for non-Russians and non-Chinese to secure top-level jobs as it is for negroes in the USA.

A few Soviet Jews have been allowed

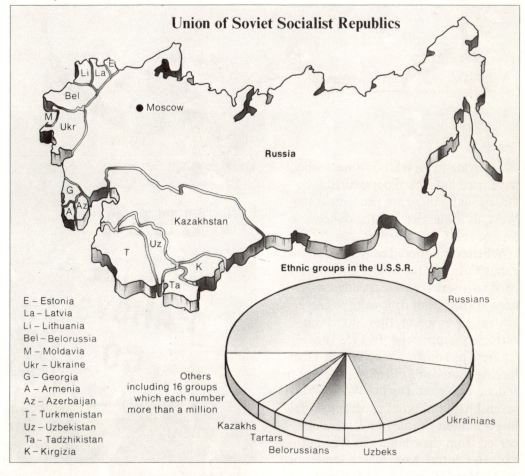

### Union of Soviet Socialist Republics

Moscow

Russia

Kazakhstan

E – Estonia
La – Latvia
Li – Lithuania
Bel – Belorussia
M – Moldavia
Ukr – Ukraine
G – Georgia
A – Armenia
Az – Azerbaijan
T – Turkmenistan
Uz – Uzbekistan
Ta – Tadzhikistan
K – Kirgizia

**Ethnic groups in the U.S.S.R.**

Russians

Others including 16 groups which each number more than a million

Kazakhs
Tartars
Belorussians
Uzbeks
Ukrainians

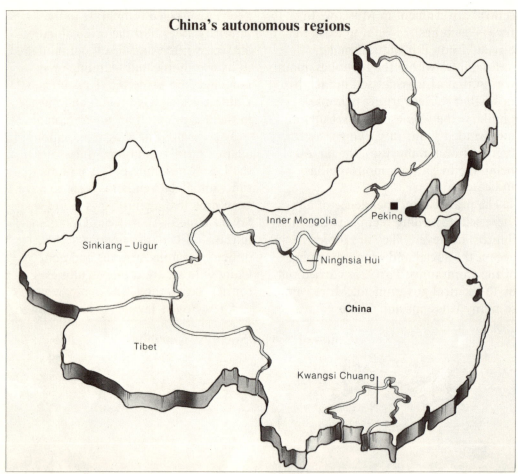

**China's autonomous regions**

Sinkiang – Uigur

Inner Mongolia

Peking

Ninghsia Hui

China

Tibet

Kwangsi Chuang

to emigrate to Israel, but others who have tried have been persecuted. Occasionally there are protests in the West, as in the cases of the dancers Valery and Galina Panov.

Whenever national minorities in either China or the Soviet Union have tried to assert their independence or been suspected of disloyalty to the central government, they have been ruthlessly suppressed. In 1959 the Chinese put down a rebellion in Tibet forcing thousands of refugees to flee to India and Nepal. During World War II several national groups, perhaps totalling a million people in all, were dispersed from their homes in Russia to exile in Central Asia, where some, such as the Volga Germans, still remain.

Tibetan refugees in Nepal

# America's Negro population – 'Freedmen but not free men'?

*'Male, Caucasian, 6 feet, 190 lbs . . .'*
This could be part of a personal description from a police or other official file in the USA. Note the use of the word *Caucasian*, meaning white. As is now largely the case in China, though not in the Soviet Union, virtually all the inhabitants of the USA speak the same language. But there is a fundamental division between white and coloured people. Non-whites include the most recent arrivals of all in the USA, refugees from Vietnam, as well as the original inhabitants of the continent, the American Indians, and the Negroes. The sorry plight of the American Indians in the reservations, where they are now penned, has been highlighted by incidents such as that at Wounded Knee, where Indians staged a protest in 1973. By far the largest coloured minority in the USA, however, are the Negroes, descendents of the slaves brought from Africa to work on the plantations of the Deep South.

*'Marriage is forbidden between white and coloured persons.'*
This is still a state law in Arizona and

Facets of the USA: Red Indian militancy (above); Vietnamese refugees (below)

# Distribution of racial groups in the U.S.A.

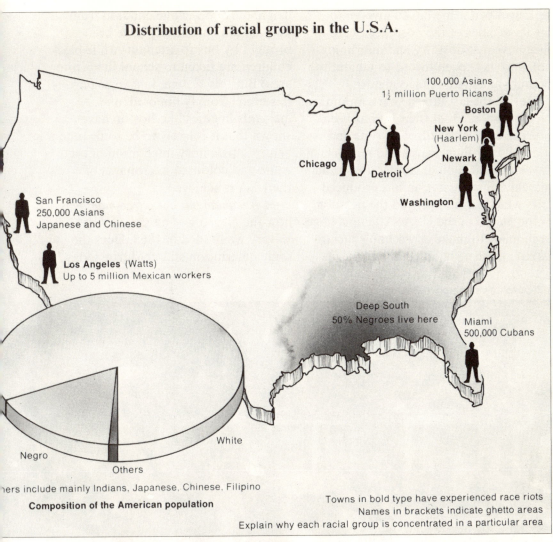

100,000 Asians
1½ million Puerto Ricans

**Boston**

**New York**
(Haarlem)

Chicago

Detroit

**Newark**

**Washington**

San Francisco
250,000 Asians
Japanese and Chinese

Los Angeles (Watts)
Up to 5 million Mexican workers

Deep South
50% Negroes live here

Miami
500,000 Cubans

White

Negro

Others

...ners include mainly Indians, Japanese, Chinese, Filipino

**Composition of the American population**

Towns in bold type have experienced race riots
Names in brackets indicate ghetto areas
Explain why each racial group is concentrated in a particular area

Virginia. It is a remnant of a whole mass of legislation and practices, that until relatively recently aimed at segregating black and white people in many parts of the USA. Officially Negroes now enjoy the same civil and political rights as white citizens, and a few of their number have reached prominent positions. But Negroes still form the largest under-privileged section of American society. More than half continue to live in the Deep South in conditions of poverty, social segregation and sometimes even persecution. Others seeking a better life have moved into the large cities of the north, but here too they have met hostility and discrimination and have been forced to inhabit the poorer slum areas, called ghettos.

During the last fifteen years, mounting Negro discontent at their lot has been expressed violently through riots and Black Power movements and more peacefully through demonstrations and marches. Such agitation has produced laws which have improved the position of the Negro in the USA. Attempts have been made to make city schools racially mixed; when a school is in a black neighbourhood, white children from another part of the city have been brought by bus to attend it, while black children are taken to school in a white area. But this system, known as *bussing*, has been strongly opposed, and incidents in cities like Boston have shown that it is likely to be some time before satisfactory integration of the white and coloured inhabitants of the USA is achieved.

*'A freedman but not a free man'* was how the Negro was described when slavery was ended in 1865. Does the same description still hold true today?

Anti-bussing campaign in Boston

BENJ DEAN - HART - PERRY - PATK F GAVIN
SOUTH BOSTON HIGH SCHOOL

MY GRANDCHILDREN ARE DENIED
THE RIGHT TO ATTEND THE SCHOOLS
THEIR PARENTS AND GRANDPARENTS
ATTENDED

STOP FORCED BUSSING

Faces of Black America: race riots (*above*) and Vietnam (*below*).

# The American Civil War

Substantially the super-powers had acquired their present shape and size by the latter half of the nineteenth century. But before each could be welded together under the form of government we know today each in turn had to undergo the traumatic experience of civil war.

In the USA this occurred between 1861 and 1865, when eleven southern states known as the Confederacy sought to leave the rest of the Union and set themselves up as a separate country, in which negroes would remain as slaves. The main events of what has been described as '*the world's first modern war*' are detailed on the map. Notice also the 'modern' aspects illustrated. The inevitable victory of the industrial north secured the future of the USA as a united country and the freedom of its negro population from slavery.

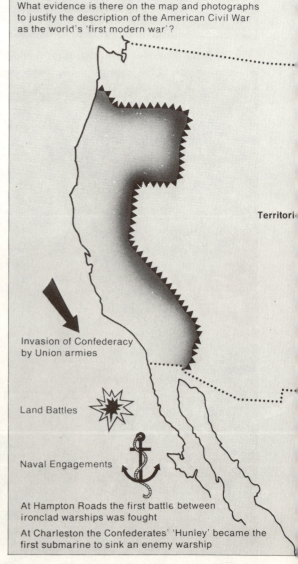

What evidence is there on the map and photographs to justify the description of the American Civil War as the world's 'first modern war'?

Territori

Invasion of Confederacy by Union armies

Land Battles

Naval Engagements

At Hampton Roads the first battle between ironclad warships was fought

At Charleston the Confederates' 'Hunley' became the first submarine to sink an enemy warship

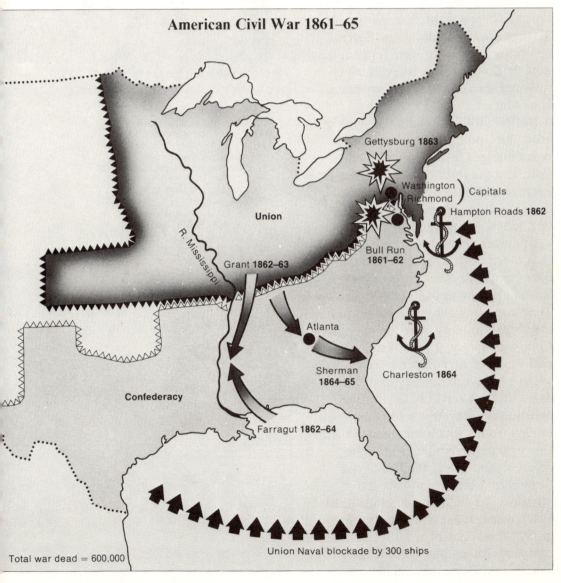

# American Civil War 1861–65

Gettysburg **1863**

Washington
Richmond } Capitals

Hampton Roads **1862**

Bull Run
**1861–62**

**Union**

R. Mississippi

Grant **1862–63**

Atlanta

Sherman
**1864–65**

Charleston **1864**

**Confederacy**

Farragut **1862–64**

Total war dead = 600,000

Union Naval blockade by 300 ships

# The Russian Revolution

In 1861, the year which saw the outbreak of the American Civil War, the serfs in Russia were freed from conditions of slavery, similar to those which shackled the negro in the USA. But Russian society and government remained semi-feudal in nature with ultimate power resting in the hands of the Tsar. During the later years of the nineteenth century and the early ones of the twentieth, the country seethed with unrest. There were strikes, plots, assassinations and uprisings. Several revolutionary parties were formed, most notably that of the Bolsheviks which followed the Communist doctrines of Karl Marx.

In 1917, Russia was on the verge of economic and military collapse after being plunged into the First World War, and the Bolsheviks seized power. Early in the morning of 7th November, their forces, prompted by Lenin and directed by Trotsky, occupied all the key points in Petrograd* and arrested the government. They quickly extended their control to other parts of the Russian heartland including Moscow. Their coup was almost bloodless but, as they began to reorganize the state along Communist lines, it provoked a bloody civil war. For two desperate years, from 1918 to 1920, the Bolsheviks or Reds defended their territory against the anti-Bolshevik or White forces and foreign troops which surrounded them. One by one the White armies were defeated, and finally the Bolsheviks themselves were able to take the offensive. When their soldiers entered Vladivostok, the last White stronghold, in 1922 their control of all Russia was complete. Russia had become the world's first Communist state.

\* Formerly St Petersburg and now Leningrad

Tsar Nicholas II and his family in 1917

**Revolution 1917**

| | |
|---|---|
| February | – Revolution breaks out |
| March | – Tsar abdicates |
| April | – Lenin returns from exile |
| November | – Bolshevik coup |
| December | – Russo-German armistice |

**Civil War 1918–22**

| | |
|---|---|
| 1918 | – Advance of Czech Legion halted |
| 1919 | – Kolchak defeated |
| | – Yudenich withdraws |
| | – Denikin resigns command |
| 1920 | – Withdrawal of Americans, British and French |
| | – Pilsudski defeated |
| | – Red Army takes offensive |
| 1921 | – Bolsheviks gain control of Transcaucasia and Turkestan |
| 1922 | – Bolsheviks enter Vladivostok |

White Armies and Interventionist Forces

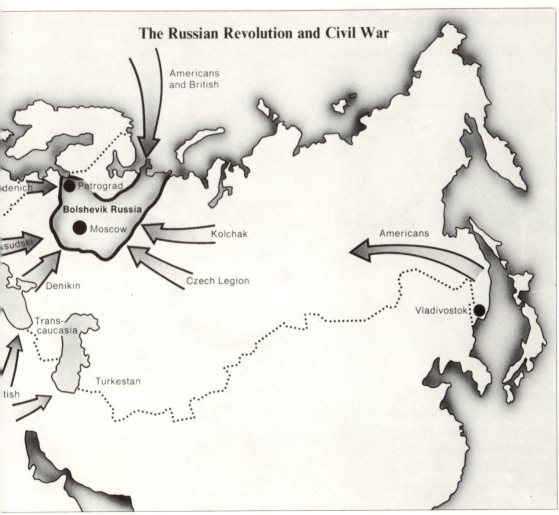

## The Russian Revolution and Civil War

Americans
and British

denich

Petrograd

**Bolshevik Russia**

Moscow

Kolchak

sudski

Denikin

Czech Legion

Americans

Trans-
caucasia

Vladivostok

Turkestan

tish

# China's Communist take-over

*'If we don't put our foot on the egg we shall have to chase the chicken around the farmyards of the world.'*
So said Winston Churchill in 1918, arguing that the British and Americans should intervene to crush the Bolsheviks in Russia. Certainly it was not long before the Russian Revolution had a profound impact on China. Here the last great dynasty, that of the Manchus, had been overthrown in 1911 and a republic proclaimed. But soon China

was thrown into chaos by the feuds of the warlords, who rampaged over the countryside with their private armies like mediaeval barons. It was the Russians who urged the new Chinese Communist Party to unite with the Nationalists (Republicans) to crush the warlords, and who helped to reorganize their forces to enable them to do so.

Any alliance between Nationalists and Communists in China, however, could only be temporary. For the Nationalists were the party of the middle class, while the Communists represented the workers and peasants.

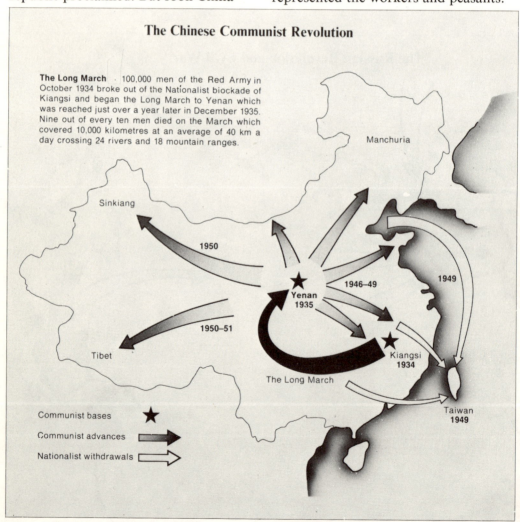

**The Chinese Communist Revolution**

**The Long March** · 100,000 men of the Red Army in October 1934 broke out of the Nationalist blockade of Kiangsi and began the Long March to Yenan which was reached just over a year later in December 1935. Nine out of every ten men died on the March which covered 10,000 kilometres at an average of 40 km a day crossing 24 rivers and 18 mountain ranges.

Manchuria

Sinkiang

1950

Yenan
1935

1946–49

1949

1950–51

Tibet

Kiangsi
1934

The Long March

Taiwan
1949

Communist bases ★
Communist advances ➡
Nationalist withdrawals ⇨

Civil war broke out in 1926. With much inferior forces, the Communists were forced to take refuge first in the hills of southern China and later, after the Long March, in the uplands and caves of the north, close to the Soviet border. From this base, under the leadership of Mao Tse-tung, they waged an incessant guerrilla war, gaining steadily in strength and support. By 1949 they were able to sweep south and win control of the whole of mainland China, forcing the remnants of the Nationalist forces to flee to the island of Taiwan.

Mao on the Long March; re-enacted by China's Young Pioneers (below)

## Communism versus capitalism

Thus, by the middle of the twentieth century, the USSR, the largest state in the world, and China, the most populous, were controlled by Communist governments committed to spread communism to the rest of the globe.

The USA, the most highly developed nation in the world and believing in the totally different system of capitalism, was equally committed to resist any such spread. Here lay the germs of a possible global conflict.

A Chinese poster attacks the American enemy; President L. B. Johnson

## Further reading and reference

*A Concise History of East Asia*
C P Fitzgerald · Penguin

*The Birth of Communist China*
C P Fitzgerald · Penguin

*Red Star Over China*
Edgar Snow · Penguin

*The Making of Modern Russia*
L Kochan · Penguin

*A Map History of Russia*
B Catchpole · Heinemann

*Ten Days That Shook The World*
John Reed · Penguin

*A Map History of the United States*
B Catchpole · Heinemann

*The Pelican History of the United States – Vol. 3*
W R Brock · Penguin

*The American Civil War*
W Churchill · Corgi

*The Autobiography of Miss Jane Pitman*
E J Gaines · Bantam

*Go Tell It On The Mountain*
James Baldwin · Corgi

*Behind Ghetto Walls*
L Rainwater · Penguin

*Atlas of World History*
(two volumes)
Penguin

*China – an Integrated Study*
A Cotterell and D Morgan · Harrap

## Terminology

Check the definitions or explanations of each of the following terms:

| | |
|---|---|
| Permafrost | discrimination |
| taiga | segregation |
| tundra | bussing |
| autocratic | serfs |
| steppes | feudal |
| federal | coup |
| ethnic | dynasty |
| annex | warlords |
| autonomous | guerrilla |

## Seminars

Prepare brief seminars on the following key figures in the historical development of the super-powers:

China
Emperor C'hin
Confucius
Sun Yat-sen
Chiang Kai-shek

USSR
Ivan the Terrible
Peter the Great
Karl Marx
Trotsky

USA
George Washington
Thomas Jefferson
Abraham Lincoln
Woodrow Wilson

## Discussion

**1** *'Imperialists who denounce American imperialism.'*
Do you think that there is any truth in

this view of China and the Soviet Union?

**2** *'We hold these truths to be self-evident, that all men are created equal, that they are endowed by their Creator with certain inalienable rights, that among these are life, liberty and the pursuit of happiness.'*
This is the opening statement of America's Declaration of Independence made in 1776. How far do you consider its sentiments have been fulfilled in the USA in the last two hundred years?

**3** When he was awarded an Oscar as the best film actor of 1972 Marlon Brando refused to accept it and sent an Indian girl to explain why. He was protesting at the way in which Indians had been treated in America in general and depicted in films in particular. Do you think that he had a good case?

**4** *'In the interests of progress minority cultures must be submerged in that of the majority.'*
How far would you support this view with reference to the super-powers and Britain?

**5** *'You can't legislate for racial integration.'*
What does this mean? Is it fair comment?

**6** *'Chinese contempt for foreigners, Russian acceptance of dictatorship and American obsession with individual liberty can all be explained by history.'*
How far do you agree?

**Mirrors of society**

Literature and music reflect the time and society which produced them. Therefore, books, films and popular

Gesture of solidarity: actor Marlon Brando sends an Indian girl to reject his Oscar award

| Title of work | Type of work | Author, Director etc. | Main features of work including period and conditions depicted |
|---|---|---|---|
| War and Peace | | | |
| Gone With The Wind | | | |
| Blues | | | |
| Ivan the Terrible | | | |
| Birth of a Nation | | | |
| Dr Zhivago | | | |
| The Small Woman | | | |
| Uncle Tom's Cabin | | | |
| Huckleberry Finn and Tom Sawyer | | | |
| Spirituals | | | |
| Battleship Potëmkin | | | |

music can aid understanding of some of the events described in the text. Try to read, watch or listen to as many of the following as possible and fill in the details concerning each in a table like the one above. (Note that many books have been filmed or serialized on television.)

## Dissertation theme

Compile an outline history of the Negro in the USA using the headings:– Slave Trade; Slavery in the Deep South; American Civil War; Carpet-Baggers and the Klu Klux Klan; Struggle for Civil Rights; Black Power; Position Today.

## Sidelights

1 Note down the national flags, emblems and anthems of each super-power. How do these reflect the history or outlook of each state?

2 What is the significance of the following dates:–
a 1st May in the USSR and China?
b 4th July in the USA?

3 In what ways do you think the terms *Uncle Sam* and *Mother Russia* reflect American and Russian attitudes towards their countries?

# Communism and capitalism

## The structure of the state

Do these men still hold the fate of the world in their hands? If they are still the leaders of the super-powers, as you read this, the answer is, 'yes'. For as men who have risen to positions of supreme authority in the super-powers, they are also the men who would press the button to trigger off a nuclear holocaust. The broad base of government is different in each super-power. China is a unitary state for instance. There are federal administrations in the USSR and USA, with the 50 states in the USA enjoying a considerable amount of real control over their own affairs. But in each of the three powers, both the day to day and the long-term business of government has devolved upon a small but powerful cabinet, dominated by a president or prime minister.

President Leonid Brezhnev, USSR

President Jimmy Carter, USA

In the USA the President and his cabinet cannot actually make laws; only the Congress can do this. Theoretically the cabinets in the USSR and China are similarly limited, but in fact they do make policy, as the Supreme Soviet and National Peoples' Congress respectively are too large and meet too rarely to exert much effective authority. Both these legislative assemblies and the smaller bodies, which they appoint to act on their behalf, do little more in practice than function as rubber stamps for laws already put into effect by the cabinet. In reality of course all agencies of government in China and the USSR are merely carrying out policies laid down by the ruling Communist parties.

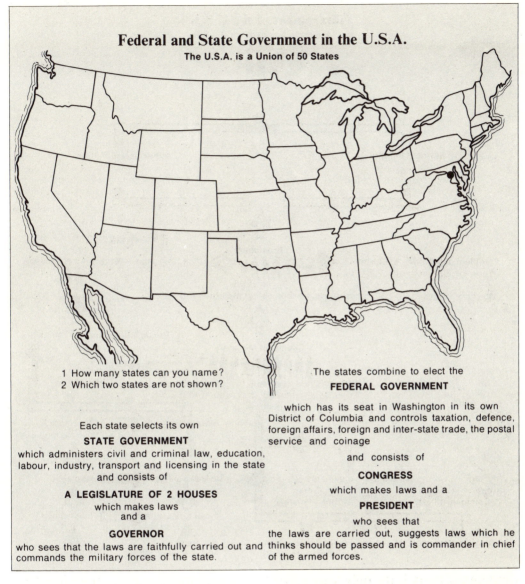

## Federal and State Government in the U.S.A.
### The U.S.A. is a Union of 50 States

1 How many states can you name?
2 Which two states are not shown?

Each state selects its own

**STATE GOVERNMENT**

which administers civil and criminal law, education, labour, industry, transport and licensing in the state and consists of

**A LEGISLATURE OF 2 HOUSES**
which makes laws
and a

**GOVERNOR**

who sees that the laws are faithfully carried out and commands the military forces of the state.

The states combine to elect the

**FEDERAL GOVERNMENT**

which has its seat in Washington in its own District of Columbia and controls taxation, defence, foreign affairs, foreign and inter-state trade, the postal service and coinage

and consists of

**CONGRESS**

which makes laws and a

**PRESIDENT**

who sees that the laws are carried out, suggests laws which he thinks should be passed and is commander in chief of the armed forces.

# The Communist Party machine

'*The Communists*', said Karl Marx, '*are . . . the most advanced and resolute section of the working-class parties of every country, that section which pushes forward all others; . . . they have over the great mass of the proletariat the advantage of clearly understanding the line of march . . . of the proletarian movement.*' Lenin viewed the Communist Party in Russia as the '*vanguard of the Proletariat*', an elite body whose sacred mission was to lead the mass of the people to achieve a fully communist society. To do this the Party had to dominate both the government and the minds of the people.

So, although it contains only 6 per cent of the total population (about 15 million people altogether) the

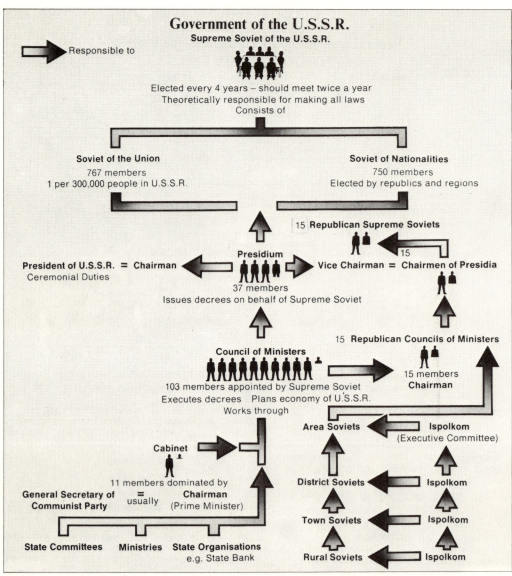

# Government of the U.S.S.R.

**Supreme Soviet of the U.S.S.R.**

Elected every 4 years – should meet twice a year
Theoretically responsible for making all laws
Consists of

**Soviet of the Union**
767 members
1 per 300,000 people in U.S.S.R.

**Soviet of Nationalities**
750 members
Elected by republics and regions

**Responsible to**

**15 Republican Supreme Soviets**

**President of U.S.S.R. = Chairman**
Ceremonial Duties

**Presidium**
37 members
Issues decrees on behalf of Supreme Soviet

**15 Vice Chairman = Chairmen of Presidia**

**15 Republican Councils of Ministers**

**Council of Ministers**
103 members appointed by Supreme Soviet
Executes decrees   Plans economy of U.S.S.R.
Works through

15 members
**Chairman**

**Cabinet**
11 members dominated by

**General Secretary of Communist Party** = usually **Chairman** (Prime Minister)

**State Committees   Ministries   State Organisations**
e.g. State Bank

**Area Soviets** ← **Ispolkom** (Executive Committee)
**District Soviets** ← **Ispolkom**
**Town Soviets** ← **Ispolkom**
**Rural Soviets** ← **Ispolkom**

Communist Party is the only legal party in the USSR. At a general or local election in the Soviet Union, all the candidates are either a member of the Communist Party or have been approved by it. In fact only one candidate is ever presented in each constituency. Voters can register their disapproval by striking out the candidate's name on the ballot paper, but by doing this they are likely to draw unwelcome attention to themselves.

Consequently, Soviet elections invariably show an almost 100 per cent vote in favour of the Communist Party, indicating, according to the Soviets, how united their people are compared to those in capitalist countries like the USA, where people are divided by class and wealth. You can decide how seriously such a claim should be taken.

With a membership of some 20 million people (comprising about 3 per cent of the total population) the

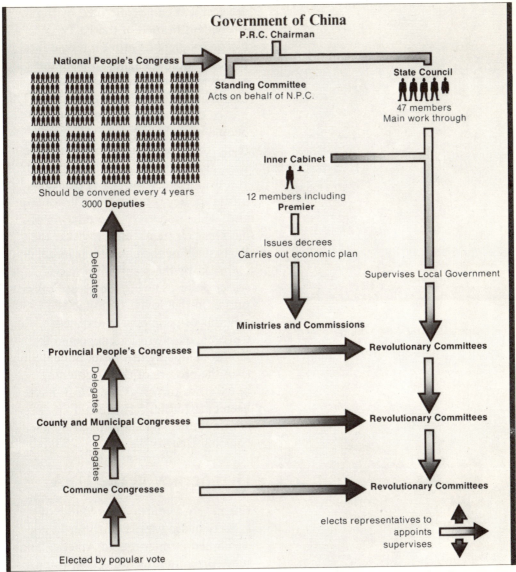

**Government of China**

P.R.C. Chairman

National People's Congress

Standing Committee
Acts on behalf of N.P.C.

State Council
47 members
Main work through

Inner Cabinet
12 members including
Premier

Issues decrees
Carries out economic plan

Should be convened every 4 years
3000 **Deputies**

Delegates

Supervises Local Government

Ministries and Commissions

Provincial People's Congresses → Revolutionary Committees

Delegates

County and Municipal Congresses → Revolutionary Committees

Delegates

Commune Congresses → Revolutionary Committees

elects representatives to
appoints
supervises

Elected by popular vote

Communist Party in China controls elections and secures the return of candidates it nominates or approves of no less effectively than its Soviet counterpart. For the Communist Party of China also regards itself as '*a vigorous vanguard organization leading the proletariat and the revolutionary masses in the fight against the class enemy*.'

Within the governments of both China and the Soviet Union, therefore, all the key posts are held by Communists. The top Party members are also the top members of the government. All the most important government bodies in both countries are composed almost entirely of Party members. At lower levels of local and regional administration, the Party may not be so well represented, but it is still dominant. Moreover, the organization of the Party closely parallels that of the administration, so that at every level the work of

government can be directed by the equivalent branch of the Party.

To complete its grip on the country, the Communist Parties of both the USSR and China control the mass media and all aspects of education. This means that the Soviet and Chinese people are told only what their respective Communist Parties decide they should be told. No opposition to, and usually very little criticism of, official policy is tolerated. Censorship and, when necessary, the purging of dissident elements, either within the Party itself or the country at large, is enforced by the security service or secret police. During the great Stalinist purges in the Soviet Union in the 1930s, millions of people were arrested, tortured, executed and deported to labour camps by the secret police. Since then the powers of this frightening body, now known as the KGB, have been curbed but they are still considerable. In China the army itself controls security.

## Democracy in the USA

For nearly a century, the Statue of Liberty in New York harbour has welcomed immigrants to America and symbolized the freedom they would enjoy in their new homeland. In contrast to the totalitarian nature of the communist regimes in the USSR and China, the USA possesses a more open society and system of government. Freedom of speech is guaranteed by the Constitution. There are no secret police, although there has been widespread criticism of the two American security services, the FBI and the CIA, for engaging in secret activities against individuals, institutions and countries.

The Statue of Liberty, New York Harbour

# The Election and Organisation of the Federal Government of the U.S.A.

## Congressional Elections

1 Each state elects two Senators to the Senate to serve for six years. One third of the Senate must retire or stand for re-election every two years.

2 Every two years each state elects Congressmen to the House of Representatives, the number being proportional to the state's population.

## Presidential Elections

Presidential Elections are held every four years. Each state has a number of electors equal to the number of its senators and congressmen combined. The electors vote for the presidential candidate who won the most popular votes in the state. No president can serve more than two terms of office. A Vice-President is also elected with the President.

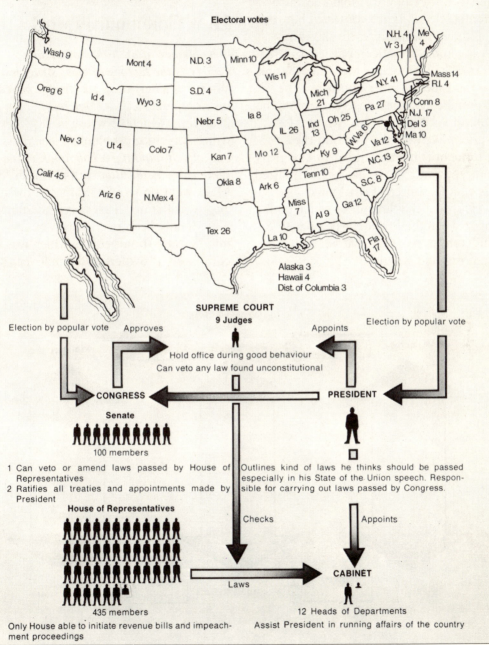

**Electoral votes**

Wash 9, Oreg 6, Mont 4, Id 4, Wyo 3, N.D. 3, S.D. 4, Nebr 5, Minn 10, Wis 11, Mich 21, N.H. 4, Me 4, Vr 3, N.Y. 41, Mass 14, R.I. 4, Nev 3, Ut 4, Colo 7, Kan 7, Ia 8, IL 26, Ind 13, Oh 25, Pa 27, Conn 8, N.J. 17, Del 3, Ma 10, W.Va 6, Va 12, Calif 45, Ariz 6, N.Mex 4, Okla 8, Ark 6, Mo 12, Ky 9, Tenn 10, N.C. 13, S.C. 8, Tex 26, Miss 7, Al 9, Ga 12, La 10, Fla 17

Alaska 3
Hawaii 4
Dist. of Columbia 3

**SUPREME COURT**
**9 Judges**

Election by popular vote — Approves — Appoints — Election by popular vote

Hold office during good behaviour
Can veto any law found unconstitutional

**CONGRESS** — **PRESIDENT**

**Senate**
100 members

1 Can veto or amend laws passed by House of Representatives
2 Ratifies all treaties and appointments made by President

Outlines kind of laws he thinks should be passed especially in his State of the Union speech. Responsible for carrying out laws passed by Congress.

Checks — Appoints

**House of Representatives**
435 members

Only House able to initiate revenue bills and impeachment proceedings

Laws

**CABINET**
12 Heads of Departments
Assist President in running affairs of the country

Unlike the other two super-powers, the USA is a two-party state. In the Soviet Union and China, elections are held essentially to confirm the position of the ruling Communist Parties in power. In America they are held to decide who will form the next government. Both Congressional and Presidential elections are contested between candidates who represent the Democratic and Republican parties. In broad terms the Democrats are somewhat akin to the Liberals in Britain, while the Republicans more closely resemble the Conservatives. Given a two-party system like this, the fact that the President is not a member of Congress, nor appointed by it, has been criticized as being a source of weakness.

Think of the difficulties which could arise when the President belongs to a different party from that which has a majority in Congress.

How do you get rid of a President who has behaved criminally or unconstitutionally?

Try to find out about the process of impeachment, the threat of which forced President Nixon to resign in 1974 over the Watergate affair.

## How Communism works

'*The history of all hitherto existing society is the history of class struggles.*' With this assertion Karl Marx opened his argument in *The Communist Manifesto* which he wrote in 1848, and which has since become for '*countless millions of mankind a holy book in the same class as the Bible or the Koran*'. Marx went on to explain that in the class war the upper class (aristocracy) had already been overthrown by the middle class (bourgeoisie) which was composed of owners and employers.

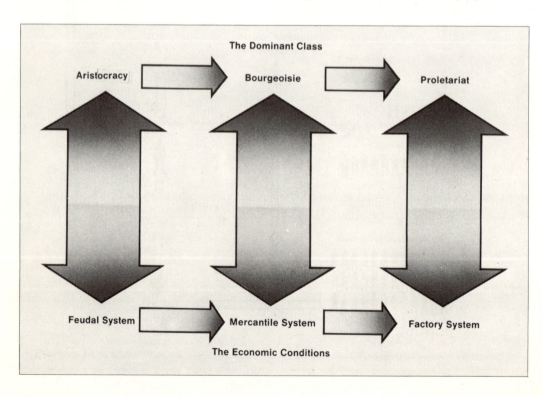

Karl Marx

Now it was the turn of the lowest class (proletariat), the workers whose labour the capitalist bourgeoisie exploited, to assume political power, by violent revolution if necessary. From the '*dictatorship of the proletariat*' would ultimately emerge the ideal classless society. So '*workers of the world unite*' was the clarion call with which Marx ended his Manifesto.

Communists have ruled the Soviet Union for over fifty years and China for more than twenty-five. What kind of progress have they made along the road to the Marxist Utopia? It can be argued that in both countries political power is in the hands of the proletariat. In the USSR this power is exercised through the right of the workers and peasants to elect their own councils or Soviets at every level of government. Peoples' Congresses and Revolutionary Committees fulfil a similar function in China. But all these bodies are domi-

nated by the Communist Party. Instead of a dictatorship of the proletariat in Russia and China, might it be more accurate to say that there is '*a dictatorship of the Communist Party over the proletariat and the dictatorship of a few individuals over the Communist Party*'?

### The proletarian programme

1  Abolition of private ownership of land and application of all rents from land to public purposes.

2  A heavy progressive or graduated income tax.

3  Abolition of all right of inheritance.

4  Confiscation of the property of all emigrants and rebels.

5  Centralization of credit in the hands of the State by means of a national bank with State capital and an exclusive monopoly.

6  Centralization of the means of transport and communication in the hands of the State.

7  Extension of factories and instruments of production owned by the State; the bringing into cultivation of wastelands, and the improvement of the soil generally in accordance with a common plan.

8  Equal liability of all to labour. Establishment of industrial armies, especially for agriculture.

9  Combination of agriculture with manufacturing industries.

10  Free education for all children in public (state) schools.

How many of these measures have been put into effect in Britain?

These are the reforms which Marx advocated that a victorious proletariat should immediately undertake. The programme has been faithfully executed in China and the USSR. The basis of the Communist economic system, as practised in both countries, is the ownership of all natural resources and all means of production equally by all the people through the state. There are no landlords or factory owners. A limited amount of private ownership is permitted, but private individuals may not employ others to work for them.

Economic development is closely controlled by the central government, which at regular intervals, usually every five years, makes a national plan. In this it works out how much money must be given to each branch of agriculture and industry, to help it achieve the production target set for it. The government also decides whereabouts in the country any new schemes are to be located and, if necessary, it will move people from one area to another to carry out this part of its plan.

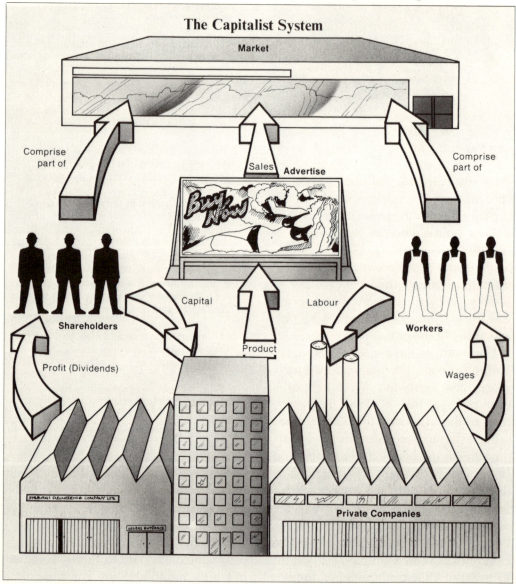

The Capitalist System

# Capitalism in action

### 'Land of the dollar bill'

Perhaps this description of the USA underlines how the pursuit of money is the driving force of American society. For can it be denied that the capitalist system as practised in America is based upon human greed – what economists call the profit motive? There is no state ownership in the USA. All goods are produced by, and all services are provided by private enterprises, ranging from those owned by individuals or families to giant companies like General Motors, which has 700,000 employees, more than the total populations of cities like Edinburgh, Manchester or Bristol. Workers are employed generally on conditions negotiated by trade unions. Capital must be raised by the owners. In the case of an individual, it might be accumulated by saving, obtained by borrowing, or simply inherited. In the case of a large company, it is provided by the people who buy shares in the ownership of the business. There are 30 million shareholders in the USA. The amount of profit made depends on how efficiently the business is organized in competition with its rivals to supply the demand of the market. After tax some profit will be reinvested to buy new machinery and so on, and the rest is taken by the owners or shareholders.

Competition and the desire for profit stimulate efficiency. That is why American capitalism is so successful, say its admirers; this is why the USA is so wealthy. But, as we shall see later, the wealth is very unequally distributed. Nor has the USA always enjoyed the prosperity which it does today. Without government planning more goods may be produced than can be bought. So prices drop, profits fall, businesses have to close down, and therefore unemployment rises. How can the unemployed afford to keep up their mortgage and hire purchase payments or even buy the daily essentials of life?

# The Great Depression

During the Great Depression (1929–33) thousands of Americans had to beg for charity on the streets. *Brother can you spare a dime?* was a popular song at the time. People wandered aimlessly over the countryside looking for jobs. One out of every five workers was unemployed. The worst-hit areas were the south-eastern farming states and the cities of the north-east. Large numbers of negroes left the plantations in the south to seek work in northern cities such as Chicago, Detroit and New York, where there was already mass unemployment.

There is always the danger, some would say the certainty, that with a capitalist system the same sort of crisis will occur again. Even today there are more than three million people jobless in the USA. Some would argue indeed that capitalism cannot function properly without a permanent pool of unemployment.

Do you agree?

If so can such a state of affairs be just? Can it be morally right anyhow for one section of society, the owners, to exploit another, the workers they employ? Do you think that with strong trade union representation such exploitation can be entirely discounted?

ЭЛЕКТРОФИКАЦИЯ

ВОЛХОВСТРОЙ ДАЕШЬ ТОК!

КОММУНИЗМ ЭТО

'Lenin and Electrification' a soviet poster (above)
and an issue of *Pravda* (below)

ПРАВДА

Орган Центрального Комитета КПСС

# Architects of the Communist powers

Lenin, Stalin and Mao have each left an indelible mark on the minds of his people and on the history of his country. Each has made a vital contribution to the development of Communism, from the theoretical basis laid down by Marx to the practical systems which operate in the USSR and China today.

It was Lenin who inspired the Communists (then called Bolsheviks) first to seize power in Russia in the November Revolution of 1917, and then to keep it in the civil war which followed. Under Lenin, Marxist theories were first translated into practice. Land, banks, transport and industry were all nationalized and the system of central planning was introduced. Lenin established in the Soviet Union the apparatus for controlling and developing a modern Communist state – a strong army, a secret police force and a well-organized party. Thus Lenin can truly be described as both founder and architect of the Communist USSR. Well might his portrait stand out each day on the front page of the Communist Party newspaper *Pravda*, while his body lies embalmed in a mausoleum in Red Square in front of the Kremlin to remind the people of the USSR of the debt which they owe him.

There is now no mention of Stalin, Lenin's successor, in the USSR. Even the places called after him have been renamed. Yet it was Stalin, using the instruments of control set up by Lenin, who transformed his country from a backward, mainly agricultural one into the second greatest industrial and military nation in the world. But imagine one out of every three people

Chinese Communist Party delegates file past the 'Founding fathers': Marx, Engels, Lenin, and Stalin

in Britain killed by some dreadful scourge. Twenty million dead – this was the frightful cost in lives of Stalin's achievement. There are no monuments to Stalin in the modern Soviet Union, but the Soviet Union itself.

If today's Soviet state has been built largely by Lenin and Stalin, then Mao Tse-tung must be regarded as the architect of modern China. It was Mao who, by leading the Red Army to victory over the Nationalists, established Communist rule in China. It was Chairman Mao who then directed Communist policy until his death in the autumn of 1976. For a time he seemed content to follow the Soviet pattern, but he soon began to tread a separate path. Sometimes the path seems to have led up a blind alley or become lost in an unchartered wasteland. For example, economic production was supposed to boom, but probably in fact it fell, during the Great Leap Forward of 1958–9 which introduced communes and 'backyard furnaces', neither of which proved a success.

During the Cultural Revolution of 1966–8, economic progress was almost completely disrupted by the violent activities of the Red Guards – thousands of young revolutionaries organized by Mao to purge the Party and the country of what he feared to be increasing bourgeoisie tendencies. Peking claims that Mao was an original thinker in the same mould as Marx and Lenin, and that Maoism in China today represents the only logical and correct continuation of the Marxist-Leninist creed. Others contend that Mao's reputation rested specifically on his success as a guerrilla leader. He was able to inspire a combination of patriotic and communist fervour amongst the Chinese peasantry.

Does Maoism in this respect constitute a blueprint for the establishment of Communism in the backward countries of the Third World?

## Further reading and reference

*The Government and Politics of Communist China*
D J Waller · Hutchinson

*The Government and Politics of the Soviet Union*
L Schapiro · Hutchinson

*The Communist Manifesto*
Marx and Engels (introduction by A J P Taylor) · Penguin

*The Marxists*
C Wright Mills · Penguin

*A Short History of Socialism*
G Lichtheim · Fontana/Collins

*To The Finland Station*
E Wilson · Fontana

*Stalin*
I Deutscher · Penguin

*A History of the Russian Secret Service*
R Deacon · New English Library

*Mao Unrehearsed*
edited by S Schram · Penguin

*The Pelican History of the United States Volume 6*    D R McCoy · Penguin

*American Capitalism*
J K Galbraith · Penguin

*The Great Crash 1929*
J K Galbraith · Penguin

*Miami and the Siege of Chicago*
N Mailer · Penguin

## Terminology

Although the meaning of most of the following terms may be obvious from the text, several can be interpreted in different ways particularly when used in ideological disputes. Try to give, therefore, as concise and comprehensive definition of each as possible.

| | |
|---|---|
| unitary | constitution |
| federal | impeachment |
| legislative | bourgeoisie |
| proletariat | Utopia |
| elite | capitalist |
| purge | totalitarian |

## Research and reflection

1    The chart opposite places the key events mentioned in the text in chronological order.

Try to find out:
a  the cause;
b  the nature;
c  the results of each event.

2    Investigate the Russian and American security services, KGB, FBI and CIA under the headings
a  origin;
b  function;
c  organization;
d  record.

3    a  Make a list of federal and unitary states in the world;
b  What historical and geographical features are particular to each group?
c  What do you consider to be the advantage and disadvantages of each system?

| Year | USA | USSR | CHINA |
|---|---|---|---|
| 1848 | | Communist Manifesto | |
| 1917 | | Bolshevik Revolution | |
| 1929 | Wall Street Crash | | |
| 1929–32 | Great Depression | | |
| 1933 | New Deal | | |
| 1936–38 | | Stalinist Purges | |
| 1949 | | | Communists Gain Power |
| 1957 | | | Hundred Flowers Movement |
| 1958 | | | Great Leap Forward |
| 1966–68 | | | Cultural Revolution |
| 1972–74 | Watergate | | |

**d** What system do you consider to be most appropriate for:
– each super-power;
– the United Kingdom?

**4 a** How are Presidential candidates selected in the USA?
**b** What advantages and disadvantages do you think the American system of government has compared to that of Britain?

**5 a** How does the organization of trade unions in the USA differ from that in Britain?
**b** Do you think that the emergence of powerful trade unions has made it more or less likely that Communism will develop in advanced capitalist countries?
**c** *'Instruments of the State whose function is the regimentation not the representation of workers.'*
Do you agree with this view of Russian trade unions? Do you think that Soviet and Western trade union leaders should meet and mix with each other?

**Discussion**

**1** How far do you agree with Marx's view of history?
**2** *'Government of the people, by the people, for the people.'*
How far do you think that this view of American democracy is justified today? Could such a description be applied to government in the USSR or China?
**3** *'From each according to his ability, to each according to his needs.'*
**a** Do you think that this Communist ideal can ever be achieved?
**b** Do you consider capitalism or Communism to be the more efficient economic system? (Consider human nature, central planning etc.)
**c** Which system would you prefer to live under?
**4** The photograph on p. 50 shows an important and all-embracing aspect of life in both the USSR and China. Instruction in the theory and practice of Communism is compulsory for all. Through the media everybody is also constantly bombarded with propaganda, which stresses the virtues of

Chinese workers' discussion group

Communism and the evils of every other system. This is known as indoctrination or brainwashing.

**a** How would you justify or denounce such a system?

**b** *'Communist brainwashing is no more effective and certainly less subtle than the indoctrination of Americans (and Britons) by a capitalist-controlled media.'*

Do you agree? How far are your beliefs conditioned by what you read, hear and see every day? Do you think that political ideology should be taught in schools?

**c** Do you accept the view that compulsory religious education in schools is a form of brainwashing?

**d** Marx described religion as 'the opium of the masses'. What do you think he meant? Why are the communist regimes of China and the USSR generally hostile to religion?

### Analysis

**1** Try to find copies of
   – the American Constitution written in 1787;
   – the Communist Manifesto written in 1848.

**a** How well do you think that each has stood the test of time?

**b** What do you regard as their main strengths and weaknesses?

**2** **a** Set out the British system of government in diagram form.

**b** Itemize those features of the unwritten British Constitution which you consider to be most important.

**c** Itemize those features of both communism and capitalism which you think Britain incorporates. Do you think that the two systems can be successfully fused?

**3** It has been argued that the experience of the Russian Revolution is largely irrelevant to world communism today, and that all future Marxist revolutions will be along Maoist lines. Examine the validity of this view by:
**a** comparing the natures of the Russian and Chinese Revolutions;
**b** analyzing the nature of all other communist revolutions in the world;
**c** assessing the likelihood of where future Marxist revolutions may occur.

## Seminars

Prepare individual or group seminars on the following key figures in the twentieth century development of the super-powers:
Franklin D Roosevelt
Harry S Truman
Lenin
Stalin
Mao Tse-tung
Chou En-lai

Russian workers take to the street in protest, 1917

# Wealth and strength

## The creation of collectives

In the summer of 1929, a three-year reign of terror began in the Russian countryside. Areas like the steppes, which centuries before had been ravaged by the Tartar and Mongol hordes, once again became the scene of savage repression. Now strong-arm Communist squads arrived and, with the aid of landless peasants, police and troops, began to force the peasant farmers (kulaks) to join their small farms together to form large collective ones. Rather than do this, the kulaks burnt their crops, slaughtered their animals and destroyed their homes. Millions of them died of starvation; millions more were deported like slaves to forced labour camps in Siberia. When the terror was over, the population of many areas had been decimated, but 14 million peasant families had been absorbed into collective farms like that shown below.

If the cost of collectivization in terms of human misery and material loss was so great, what did the policy achieve? First the kulaks, who could have provided serious opposition to the Communist Party, were eliminated as a class. Second many of them could be used to work in the new industries which were being set up. Above all, the small and generally inefficient peasant farms had been replaced by large-scale units, which could be run on a modern scientific basis, employing machinery supplied by the new machine-tractor stations.

Today about half the farmland in the Soviet Union is cultivated by collectives and the rest by state farms. More specialized and even larger than the collectives, the state farms are owned directly by the state, which appoints managers to run them and pays employees to work on them. Gradually they seem to be replacing collectives as the basic type of agricultural unit in the USSR – can you suggest reasons why?

A modern collective farm in Soviet Lithuania

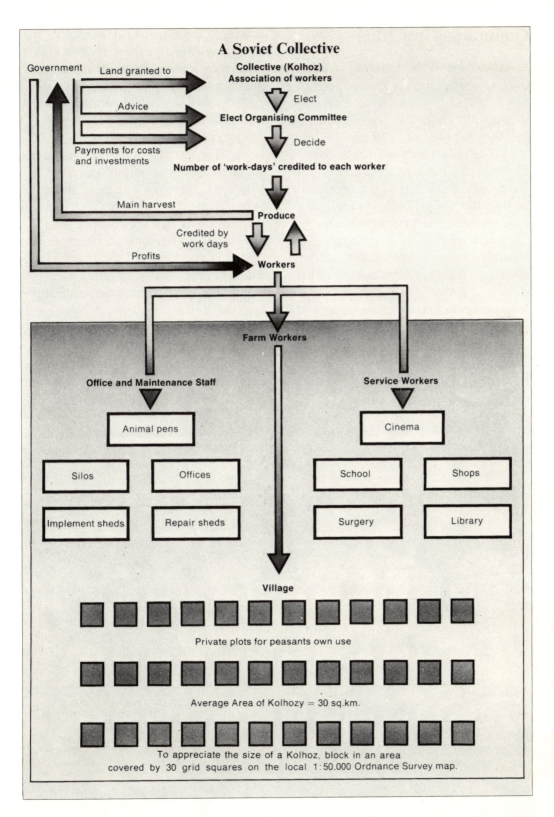

# A Soviet Collective

**Collective (Kolhoz) Association of workers**

Government — Land granted to →

— Advice →

**Elect Organising Committee**

— Payments for costs and investments →

Elect

Decide

**Number of 'work-days' credited to each worker**

Main harvest → **Produce**

Credited by work days

Profits → **Workers**

**Farm Workers**

**Office and Maintenance Staff**

| Animal pens |

| Silos | Offices |
| Implement sheds | Repair sheds |

**Service Workers**

| Cinema |

| School | Shops |
| Surgery | Library |

**Village**

Private plots for peasants own use

Average Area of Kolhozy = 30 sq.km.

To appreciate the size of a Kolhoz, block in an area covered by 30 grid squares on the local 1:50.000 Ordnance Survey map.

# Communes in China

At the time of the Communist take-over, China, as the USSR had been, was a land of peasant farmers struggling to grow just enough to feed themselves and their families on their small plots of land. The redistribution of land confiscated from the aristocracy only increased the amount of fragmentation. So, like the Soviets before them, but with less terror and disruption, the Chinese Communists introduced collective farming throughout the country. Then they went a step further still.

During the Great Leap Forward communes were established. These were formed by joining about 30 collectives together, and they were designed to work as shown in the diagram. One aim was to free women from household jobs, so that they could work in the fields. How do you think this was to be achieved? As originally planned the communes were not a success. Bearing human nature in mind, perhaps you can work out what features the peasants objected to so strongly. Certainly now that their size has been reduced and the whole system greatly modified, the communes seem to be more successful.

Grain-drying in a Chinese commune, Kirin

54

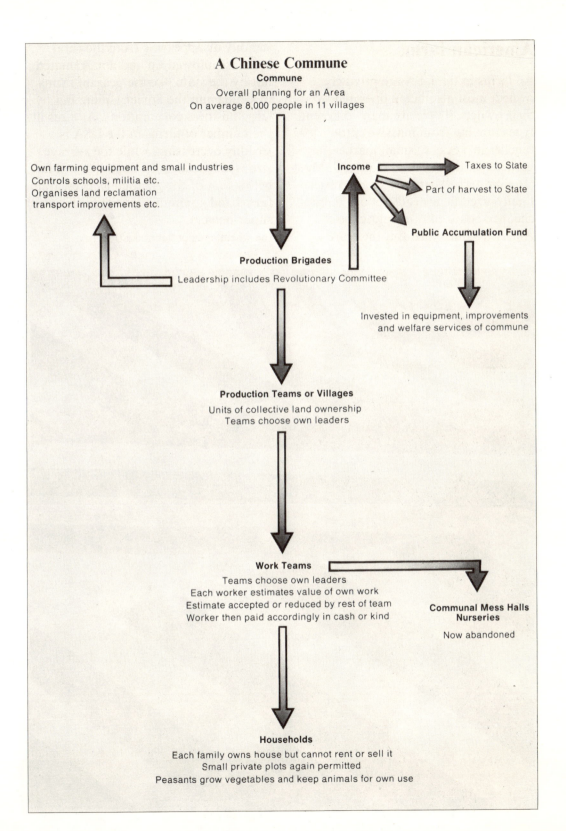

# A Chinese Commune

**Commune**

Overall planning for an Area
On average 8,000 people in 11 villages

Own farming equipment and small industries
Controls schools, militia etc.
Organises land reclamation
 transport improvements etc.

Income → Taxes to State

Part of harvest to State

**Public Accumulation Fund**

**Production Brigades**

Leadership includes Revolutionary Committee

Invested in equipment, improvements
and welfare services of commune

**Production Teams or Villages**

Units of collective land ownership
Teams choose own leaders

**Work Teams**

Teams choose own leaders
Each worker estimates value of own work
Estimate accepted or reduced by rest of team
Worker then paid accordingly in cash or kind

**Communal Mess Halls
Nurseries**

Now abandoned

**Households**

Each family owns house but cannot rent or sell it
Small private plots again permitted
Peasants grow vegetables and keep animals for own use

# American farms

All farms in the USA are privately owned, most also being operated by their owners. There are many different types ranging from massive cattle ranches in Texas to small market gardens on the Atlantic seaboard. Most familiar perhaps are the single-owner, family-sized farmsteads set out on the chequer-board prairie landscape of America's mid-west. But these are steadily disappearing from the rural scene, swallowed up and amalgamated, not by the state like the peasant farms of China and the Soviet Union, but by large business corporations. As a result, the number of farms in the USA is steadily decreasing, while the average size is increasing, although it is still far below that of the giant collectives, state farms and communes of the Communist super-powers.

The wheatlands of Nebraska USA

## Overproduction and underproduction

Are newspaper items like that below an indictment of the inefficiency of the highly-regimented, state-controlled farming systems of the Communist powers?

### Russia seeking more grain

Russia is embarking on negotiations to buy another 10 million tons of grain from North America and Australia to replenish losses on the year's harvest. The deals follow purchases of 5.2 million tons of American and Canadian wheat announced last week. The total bill for wheat, maize and barley required by Moscow will top £950 million. In Washington it was disclosed yesterday that the Kremlin's agents are making enquiries behind the scenes to buy four million tons of maize and one million of barley from American producers. The Russian grain harvest this year is now expected to plunge 25 million tons below the target figure of 215 million. Prolonged drought is ravaging crops in parts of Kazakhstan and other areas. Washington officials are maintaining that America can afford to sell 12 to 14 million tons because of record production.

Item from Sunday Telegraph – 20th July 1975

Certainly it seems ironical that the Soviet Union, not for the first time, should be forced to import food from its arch rival. It is also true that agricultural production in both the USSR and China has failed to reach the targets set for it on several occasions. In contrast, farming in the USA has for many years been producing more than has been needed. Farmers have, until recently, actually been paid not to produce as much as they could, by allowing some of their land to be permanently rested in a *soil bank*.

Only 4 per cent of the American labour force is employed in agriculture, compared with 25 per cent in the USSR and 75 per cent in China. On this basis, a farm worker in the USA can produce enough food to feed 50 other people, a peasant in the USSR only enough for 4 others, and a peasant in China little more than enough to feed himself.

Although China has undertaken a massive programme of irrigation and reclamation, it seems unlikely that there

will be any significant increase in the area of cropland in any of the three super-powers. American attempts to extend cultivation into the drier south-west produced the Dustbowl, and the new farmlands developed by the USSR in marginal Kazakhstan have suffered severe drought. Agricultural production has increased under Communist rule in both the USSR and China, but by no means as much as the planners would have liked. Can the existing farmland in these two countries ever be as efficiently used, by farmers who do not individually own the land they work on, as farmland in the USA?

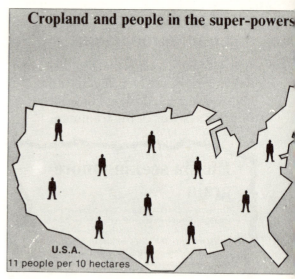

**Cropland and people in the super-powers**

U.S.A.
11 people per 10 hectares

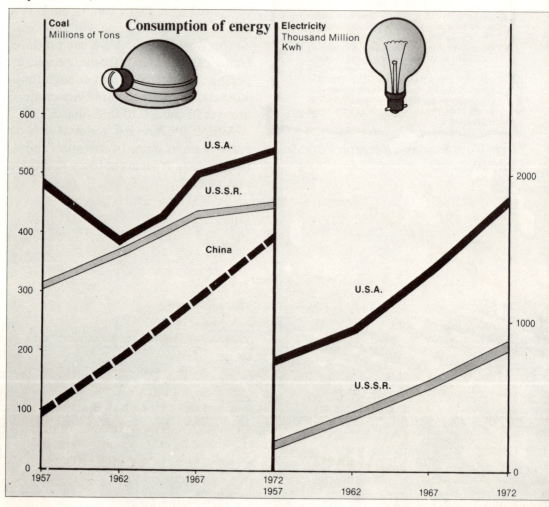

Consumption of energy

**U.S.S.R.**
10 people per 10 hectares

**China**
60 people per 10 hectares

## How much energy have they got?

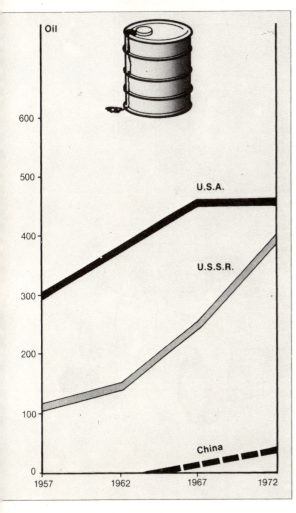

Oil

600

500

U.S.A.

400

U.S.S.R.

300

200

100

China

0

1957    1962    1967    1972

Ghost towns are now often all that remains as a witness of the gold rushes, which brought thousands of fortune-hunters flocking to California and Alaska in the nineteenth century. However, it was the discovery a little later of the 'black gold' of the oilfields, first of Pennsylvania and then of Texas and Oklahoma, which created American millionaires such as Rockefeller. Like the other two super-powers, the USA has been blessed with large deposits of a wide range of minerals. But with exploitation starting so early and demand being so great, some deposits have now been exhausted, while reserves of others are running dangerously low.

To conserve her relatively limited supplies of oil, for instance, the USA imports large quantities of petroleum from Venezuela and the Middle East. The interruption of supplies from the Middle East, as has been threatened, would seriously damage the American economy.

China and the USSR, on the other hand, are likely to be self-sufficient in their energy requirements for some time to come, and both also contain large reserves of most other important minerals. Soviet scientists have claimed that the USSR, which is larger of course than the USA and China combined, possesses huge quantities of the world's total reserves of several vital minerals.

# The industrial time-lag

Rockefeller, Carnegie, Armour, Ford, Pullman – how many of these names have you heard of? All were men who rose from being poor boys to become multi-millionaires. During the latter part of the nineteenth century they, and others like them, built up the huge business corporations that by 1900 had

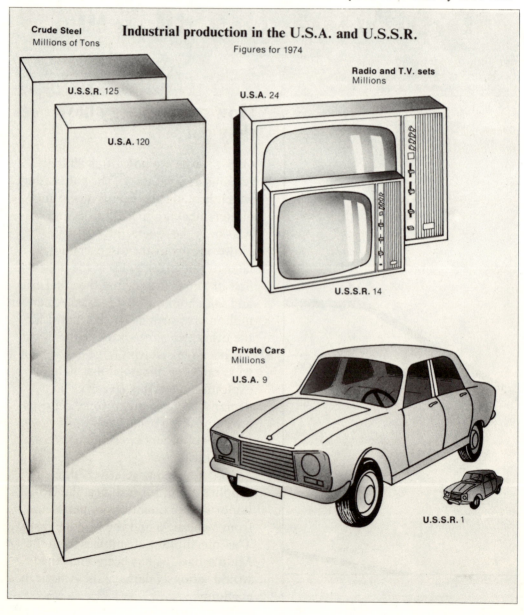

**Industrial production in the U.S.A. and U.S.S.R.**
Figures for 1974

**Crude Steel**
Millions of Tons

U.S.S.R. 125

U.S.A. 120

**Radio and T.V. sets**
Millions

U.S.A. 24

U.S.S.R. 14

**Private Cars**
Millions

U.S.A. 9

U.S.S.R. 1

transformed the USA into the world's chief industrial nation, a position which she has maintained ever since.

As the twentieth century dawned, therefore, American industry already possessed the two main features which characterize it today: It was dominated by a small number of giant firms, and it produced vast quantities of an enormous variety of commodities, ranging from heavy steel goods on the one hand to cars and gramophone records on the other.

While America was thus transformed, the Soviet Union remained mainly an agricultural country. In 1931 Stalin said: *'We are 50 or 100 years behind the advanced countries. We must make good this lag in 10 years.'* So, in the same ruthless way in which he had carried out collectivization, Stalin now spurred on industrial revolution in the Soviet Union. All the emphasis was laid upon the development of heavy industry – coal, iron, steel and engineering. By coercion, by persuasion, or with patriotic enthusiasm, men and women worked like demons to expand the existing industrial areas and create new ones east of the Urals. Living standards did not rise, but new factories, furnaces and power stations did. Dramatic results were achieved; for instance, steel production rose from under 10 million tons in 1931 to over 120 million tons by 1973. In certain branches of industry, such as iron and steel, Soviet production has now over-taken American, but it still lags far behind in the manufacture of consumer goods.

China is only now entering the stage of industrialization which the USA passed through almost 100 years ago and the USSR nearly 50 years ago. She has shown that she has the resources and the skill to join both the space and the nuclear clubs. Can her breakthrough to a period of rapid industrial expansion like that already achieved by the USA and USSR be long delayed? Has it indeed already begun?

Chinese heavy industry, Anshan

# Too many, too few

During the nineteenth century, 30 million immigrants from Europe streamed across the Atlantic and poured into America. The population of the USA increased in such a spectacular fashion, that in the early years of this century laws had to be passed to restrict further immigration. Today only about 5 per cent of Americans are foreign-born. To maintain the present standard of living, the present total population and its projected growth seem to be about right for the size and resources of the country.

With a population only one fifth greater than that of the USA, and occupying an area over twice as large, the USSR must be considered an underpopulated country. Economic development in Siberia, for instance, is undoubtedly hindered by lack of labour. Can you work out why the Russians have been making particularly strenuous efforts to fill up their 'empty' eastern lands along the Chinese border?

China was already a densely populated country before the modern American and Soviet states had even

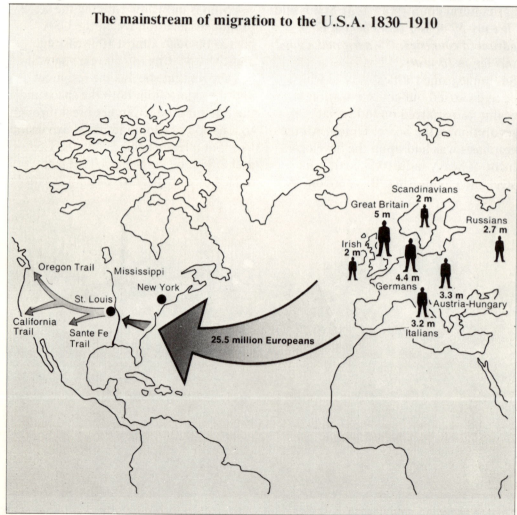

**The mainstream of migration to the U.S.A. 1830–1910**

Oregon Trail
Mississippi
New York
St. Louis
California Trail
Sante Fe Trail
25.5 million Europeans

Scandinavians 2 m
Great Britain 5 m
Russians 2.7 m
Irish 2 m
4.4 m Germans
3.3 m Austria-Hungary
3.2 m Italians

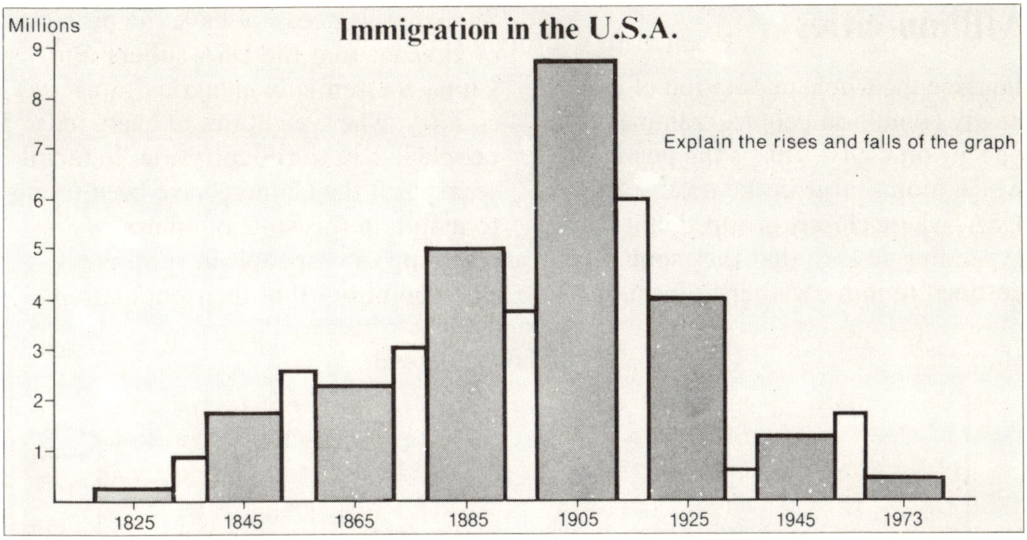
Immigration in the U.S.A.
Millions
9
8
7
6
5
4
3
2
1
Explain the rises and falls of the graph
1825
1845
1865
1885
1905
1925
1945
1973

begun to take shape. One out of every five people in the world today is Chinese. Moreover, if the present rate of population growth continues, China will have another 400 million mouths to feed in 25 years time. To achieve a uniformly high standard of living for the massive number of people they are already responsible for, and to slow down population growth, are the daunting tasks which confront the Chinese Communists.

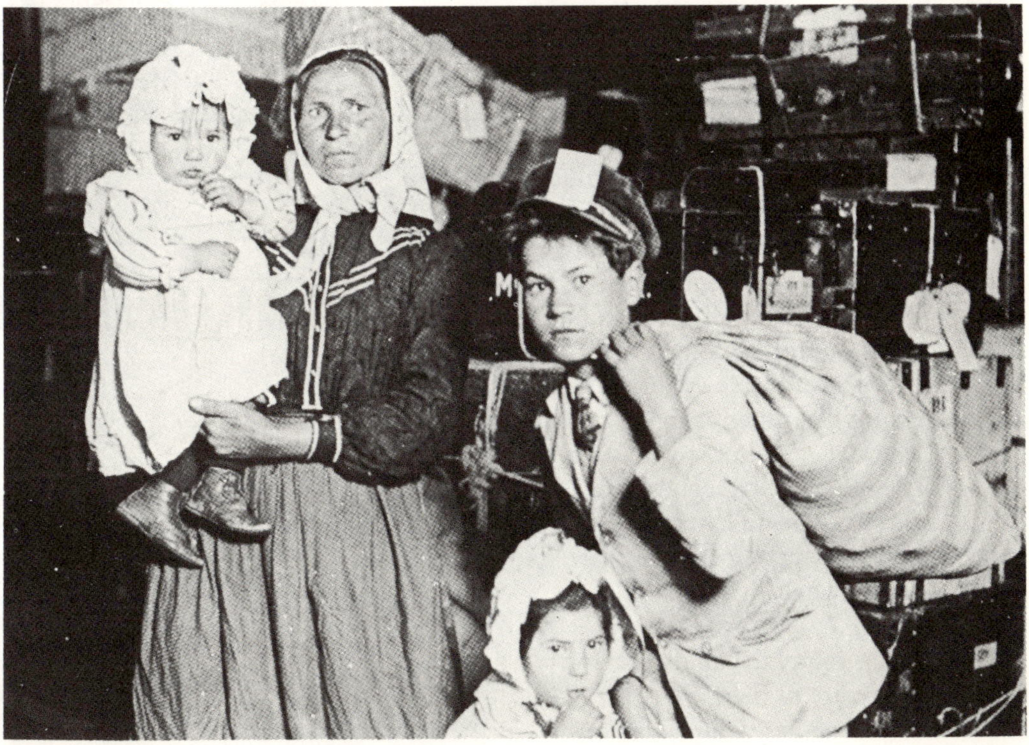

Italian immigrants entering the USA 1905

# Million-cities

Imagine the whole population of Britain, nearly 60 million people, crammed into one gigantic city. This is the possibility which looms large in the north-east USA, where closely grouped cities are expanding so fast, that they soon seem destined to join together to form one super-city called *megalopolis*. Eight out of every ten Americans live in a town. The USA is not only a land of million-aires but also of million-cities, each with its problems of slums, water supply, pollution, traffic congestion, crime and violence. In New York City alone there are five times as many murders every year as in the whole of Britain. The violence, which always seems to have permeated American society, fanned by poverty and racial hatred, is aggravated by large-scale urbanization.

There are as many urban dwellers in China as there are in the USA – about 150 million altogether. China also has its million-cities, notably Peking and Shanghai. It does not have the problem of violence that the USA suffers. But China is essentially an agricultural country, where eight out of every ten people live in the countryside. In fact it seems as if the Chinese have been trying to maintain this state of affairs by resettling townspeople in rural areas. They point out that their population

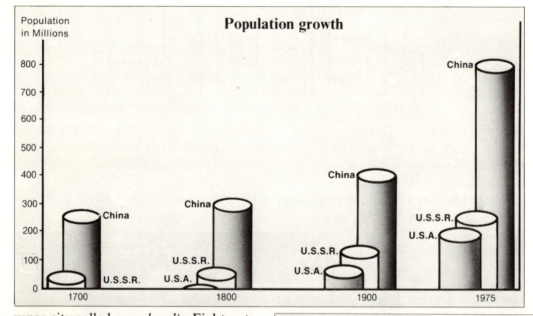

Population growth

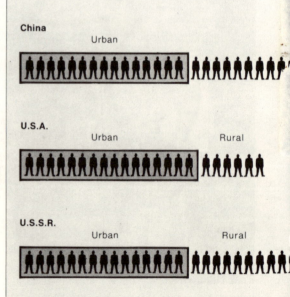

# Distribution of population

Most densely populated parts of super-powers

Cities with more than 2 million people

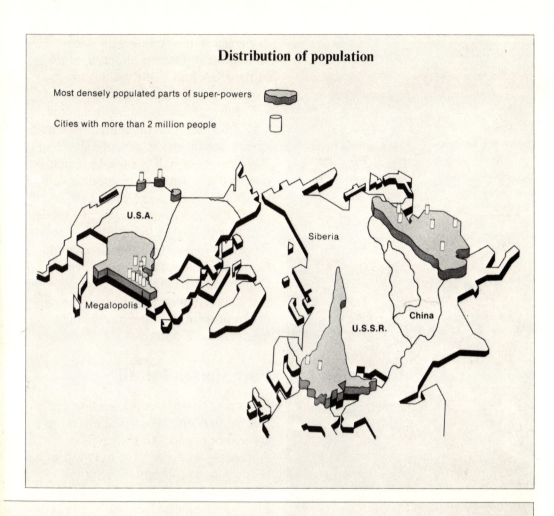

# Urban and rural population

Rural

Each figure represents 10 million people.

Los Angeles, USA

dispersed in the countryside is less vulnerable to nuclear attack than those of the USA and USSR, which are concentrated in towns and cities.

Large scale industrialization in the USSR has been accompanied by widespread urbanization. About 140 million Russians, over half the total population, now live in towns and cities, although few of the cities have attained the massive proportions of those in America. As the standard of living rises in the Soviet Union, as fewer workers labour manually, will the nature of Soviet Communism change? More specifically will a society that becomes increasingly urban in form, become increasingly bourgeoisie in outlook?

## Fair shares for all

Masses of toiling people, regimented like soldiers and all dressed alike: here is the face of modern China. The uniformity of dress is the outward sign of the classless society, which the Communists have striven to create. Even army officers wear no symbols of rank. The drabness of the clothing also reflects the low standard of living. The average Chinese has an income only about $\frac{1}{60}$ of the average American. But disease and illiteracy have been drastically reduced, and material prosperity has slowly risen under the Communist regime. Moreover, all the people have benefited equally from these improvements. Nobody now lacks the basic necessities of life. Life, it has been said, is at least 'adequate beyond the former dreams of the landless and perennially overworked, hungry illiterates who were most of the peasants in pre-revolutionary China'.

In the Soviet Union it seems as if the

people are at last beginning to enjoy the kind of prosperity promised by Marxist doctrines. With heavy industry now well established, the government is placing increasing emphasis on the production of those consumer goods which almost every American takes for granted. Even so, the national wealth of the USSR is still less than half that of the USA, and this *dollar gap* is not closing.

## A land of milk and honey

To most of us America, as depicted on our cinema and television screens, is a land overflowing with milk and honey. It produces over a third of all the goods

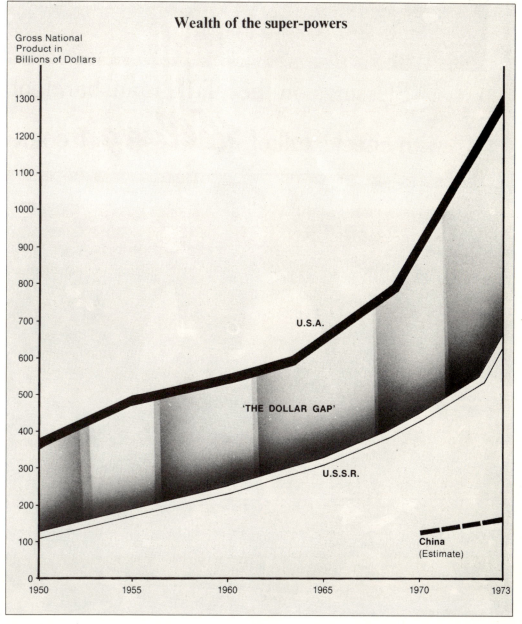

**Wealth of the super-powers**

Gross National Product in Billions of Dollars

U.S.A.

'THE DOLLAR GAP'

U.S.S.R.

China (Estimate)

and services in the world. The majority of its inhabitants enjoy a standard of living the rest of the world can only envy. But in the middle of all this wealth there is poverty. Often the two exist side by side, as in the city of Los Angeles in California, America's richest state. Throughout the USA in fact there are serious pockets of poverty. Most are in areas where the bulk of the population is coloured, but in Appalachia many poor white families depend upon government hand outs of food and money.

Such blatant inequality of wealth, and all too often of opportunity, could not exist in the USSR and China. Neither could the neglect of public and welfare services, which characterized the USA until recently and often caused distress amongst those least able to fend for themselves – the sick, the old and the handicapped. Now, however, schemes have been introduced to help the elderly and poor meet bills for medical treatment. Public amenities are being improved and welfare services expanded. Many Americans approve of such developments, as beginning to create a fairer and more humane society. Others argue that they will sap the energy and vitality of American society. You live in a welfare state. What do you think?

# Annihilation within an hour

The prospect of a nuclear war between the super-powers is almost too horrible even to think about. China only possesses a relatively limited number of nuclear weapons as yet, although she has already produced an inter-continental ballistic missile (ICBM) capable of reaching Moscow and is developing one which will be able to hit targets in the USA. Clearly she is a power to be reckoned with today and one to be feared tomorrow. The USA and USSR, it has been estimated, could virtually annihilate each other within an hour. Both possess huge stockpiles of atomic warheads hundreds of times more powerful than the bombs which destroyed Hiroshima and Nagasaki.

These warheads can be delivered to targets on the other side of the globe by electronically guided missiles, launched from silos beneath the ground or submarines beneath the sea. The flight path of these inter-continental missiles takes them out into space, and, as they re-enter the earth's atmosphere, they eject many separate warheads, each already zeroed in onto its selected target (MIRV) or capable of automatic manoeuvring (MARV). There is no effective defence against such hideous weapons, although both the USA and USSR have spent enormous sums of money installing anti-missile (ABM) systems. The only deterrent in fact is each side's certain knowledge, that if it launched a nuclear attack, it would itself be destroyed by the counter strike, which early-warning radar would have given its opponent time to get off.

Contrast in cultures (*opposite*): a street scene in New York's Haarlem district

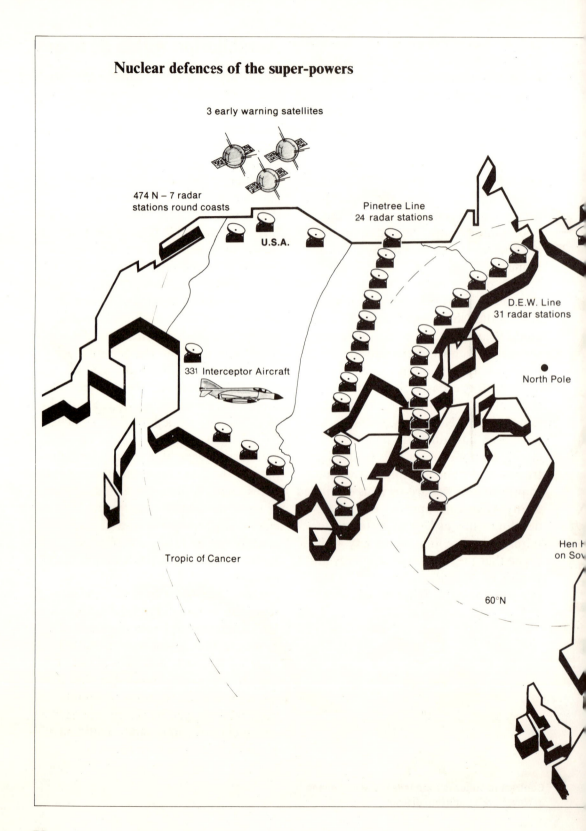

# Nuclear defences of the super-powers

3 early warning satellites

474 N – 7 radar
stations round coasts

Pinetree Line
24 radar stations

U.S.A.

D.E.W. Line
31 radar stations

North Pole

331 Interceptor Aircraft

Tropic of Cancer

Hen H
on Sov

60°N

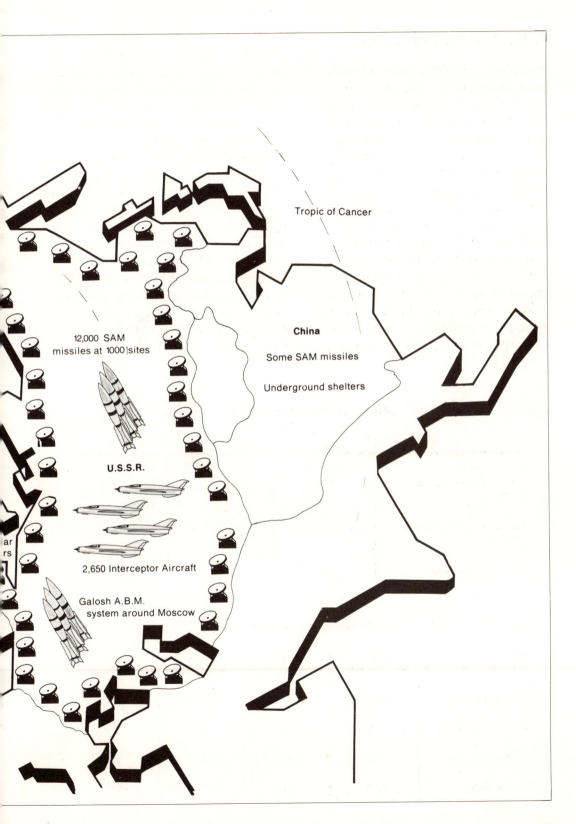

Tropic of Cancer

**China**

Some SAM missiles

Underground shelters

12,000 SAM
missiles at 1000 sites

**U.S.S.R.**

2,650 Interceptor Aircraft

Galosh A.B.M.
system around Moscow

ar
rs

# A fragile sort of peace

Peace based on the nuclear deterrent must inevitably be a fragile sort of peace. There is the ever-present danger that all-out nuclear war between the super-powers might be precipitated by an accident, or develop as a result of the escalation of a local crisis in a world flashpoint. Bearing this in mind, and burdened by the ever-increasing cost of developing new missile systems, the USA and USSR have tried to limit the arms race. At the SALT talks they agreed that no new ABM systems should be built, and that the offensive missiles each side possessed should not exceed a certain number. But no positive steps towards actual disarmament were taken.

Apart from their main nuclear armouries, all three super-powers possess huge conventional forces. The superiority of the Soviet Union in terms of overall manpower and naval strength clearly stands out. For some time, American defence chiefs have been concerned about the expansion of the Soviet fleet, particularly the submarine branch. Western experts also point with some alarm to the disparity between the military forces of the Warsaw Pact and those of NATO. They ask what would happen if the Soviet Union invaded Western Europe. With NATO unable to stem such an attack by conventional means, would the USA resort to the use of nuclear weapons and thus risk triggering off a world-wide holocaust?

## The Nuclear Armouries of the super-powers

| 1977 | U.S.A. | U.S.S.R. | China |
|---|---|---|---|
| Inter-Continental Ballistic Missiles | 1054 | 1477 | **Testing** (Some I.C.B.M. may have been deployed) |
| Submarine Launched Ballistic Missiles | 656 (41 sub-marines) | 909 (32 sub-marines) | (1 missile launching sub-marine but no missiles) |
| Long Range Bombers | 373 | 135 | About 80 medium range bombers |

## Conventional Forces

| 1977 | U.S.A. | U.S.S.R. | China | U.K. |
|---|---|---|---|---|
| Total Armed Forces | 2,088,000 | 3,675,000 | 3,950,000 | 339,150 |
| Major Combat Ships | 175 | 230 | 22 | 75 |
| Submarines | 78 | 234 | 66 | 27 |
| Combat Aircraft | 5,700 | 5,262 | 5,200 | 576 |

Military display in Moscow's Red Square

China's People's Army

# A unique army

In the USA and USSR, indeed in most countries, the armed services are clearly set apart from the rest of the population. Apart from the Red Star hat badge, it is not easy to tell soldiers from civilians, for the People's Liberation Army in China is regarded as being *one with the people*. Its $2\frac{1}{2}$ million members, backed by a huge militia, are specifically trained to resist any invading forces by fighting a *People's War*, that is a guerrilla war carried on in the countryside, where the soldiers would be supported by and be almost indistinguishable from the peasants.

As the main link between the Communist Party and mass life in China, the PLA seeks to integrate itself as closely as possible with the people. Thus at one level the army organizes schools and classes throughout the country for instructing the people in Maoist thought, while at another it runs medical centres and builds public works such as dams, power stations, irrigation canals, roads, bridges, railways and tunnels. '*How the Chinese army is used – to serve the people – is what makes it unique.*'

## Further reading and reference

*America*
Alistair Cooke · BBC Publications

*China's Long Revolution*
Edgar Snow · Penguin

*Journey into Russia*
L Van Der Post · Penguin

*The Distant Magnet*
R Taylor · Eyre & Spottiswoode

*An Economic History of the USSR*
A Nove · Penguin

*A Modern Geography of the United States*
R Estell · Penguin

*The Affluent Society*
J K Galbraith · Penguin

*The Hidden Persuaders*
V Packard · Penguin

*The Military Balance 1976–1977*
IISS

*China: The Revolution Continued*
Jon Myrdal and Gun Kessle · Penguin

*The People's Republic of China*
C Brown · Heinemann

## Discussion

**1** *'The end justifies the means.'*
Can Stalin's means be justified?

**2** *'Ordinary people in America feel involved in and not exploited by capitalism.'*
How far do you agree?

**3** *'It can never be justified,'* or *'It is a practical necessity.'*
What is your view of birth control now widely practised to limit population growth in the USA and China?

**4** *'The puritanical morality of the Communist regimes is preferable to the permissiveness of western society in general and American society in particular.'*
Do you agree? Do you think that sexual promiscuity, pop culture, increasing crime and violence etc, indicates that western society is becoming soft and decadent?

**5** *'We in the west could learn a lot from the Chinese communes.'*
Do you agree? What lessons do you think we might learn?

**6** According to an American trade union leader,
*'Western workers are being called upon to bail out the Russian economy – to save it from the catastrophe of totalitarian central planning geared to war production.'*
**a** Do you agree?
**b** Do you think that America should sell food and give technical knowledge to the Russians?

**7** *'If the benefits of commune life are no more than a full belly and a bit of cash, then the revolution in China will fail.'*
**a** What do you think this assertion means?
**b** How far do you consider that happiness can be measured by material prosperity?

**8** In China everyone who is physically able is required to spend some time doing manual labour. Do you think that this is a good idea?

**9** The law in the USSR and China has been described as 'tolerated law'. What do you think this means?

**Thoughts on the thoughts of Mao**

What is your view of the meaning and truth of each of the following dictums or assertions made by Mao Tse-tung?

*'Forget self – serve the people'*

*'Every peasant has a spontaneous desire to become a capitalist'*

*'Political power grows out of the barrel of a gun'*

*'Freedom is the recognition of necessity'*

*'The atom bomb is a paper tiger'*

*'Human will is superior to machines'*

**The literary background**

Some of the events described in the preceding chapters have stimulated or formed the actual background for well known films or books. As a group try to read or watch the following and then hold a critical discussion of them:
*The Gulag Archipelago*
*The Grapes of Wrath*
*On the Beach*
*Animal Farm*
*A Many Splendoured Thing*
*Dr Strangelove*

*The Manchurian Candidate*
*One Day in the Life of Ivan Denisovich*
*The Case of Comrade Tuloyev*
*Go Down Moses*
*Darkness at Noon*
*Nineteen Eighty-Four*

**Analysis**

Investigate the problem of violence in American society considering:
**a** its history – eg outlaws of the old west, Chicago gangsters, political assassinations etc;
**b** its causes – eg racial hatred, inequalities of wealth, right to possess firearms etc.

**War games**

Imagine situations which could occur in the world and lead to a direct confrontation between the super-powers – eg border incidents between East and West Germany, an invasion of South by North Korea, the refusal of Middle East countries to supply the USA with oil. With teams representing the super-powers play out moves that could be made, until one power would have to give way or resort to nuclear war.

# International relations

## The spectre of Communism

'*A spectre is haunting Europe, the spectre of Communism*',
wrote Marx in 1848. A hundred years later he may well have claimed that the same ghost was turning America's dream into a nightmare. During World War II the USA and USSR had fought as allies to help crush the evil of Nazi Germany. The Americans believed that they could continue to co-operate with the Russians once the war was over. Their illusions were soon shattered. The Russians refused to allow American aid into Eastern Europe, which was still occupied by the Red Army. In Winston Churchill's famous words '*an iron curtain had descended across the European continent*'.

Highly suspicious of Soviet intentions in Persia and the Eastern Mediterranean, and confronted by open hostility during the Berlin Blockade of 1948, the USA was further alarmed in 1949 when the

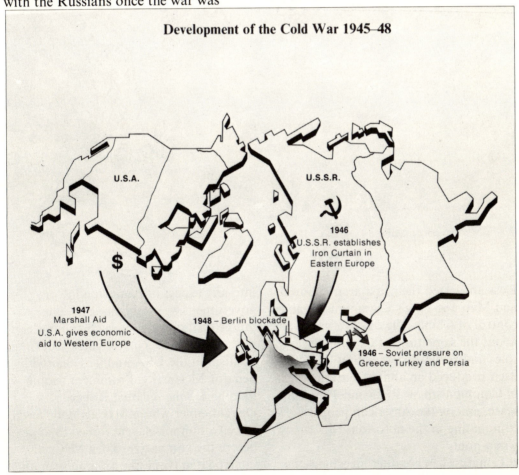

**Development of the Cold War 1945–48**

U.S.A.

U.S.S.R.

1946
U.S.S.R. establishes
Iron Curtain in
Eastern Europe

$

1947
Marshall Aid
U.S.A. gives economic
aid to Western Europe

1948 – Berlin blockade

1946 – Soviet pressure on
Greece, Turkey and Persia

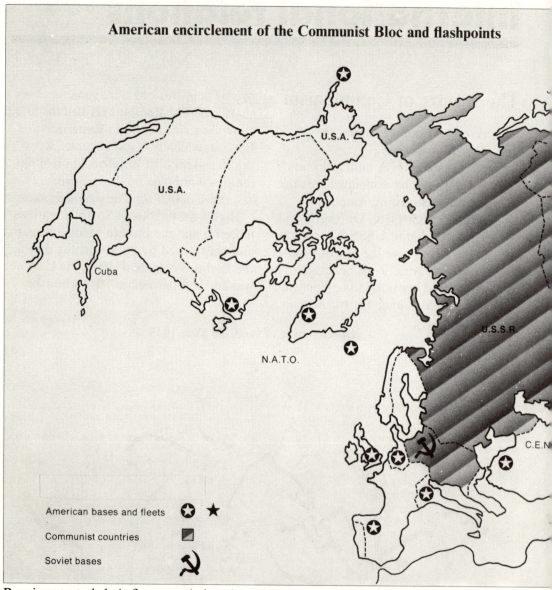

## American encirclement of the Communist Bloc and flashpoints

U.S.A.

U.S.A.

Cuba

N.A.T.O.

U.S.S.R.

C.E.N

American bases and fleets

Communist countries

Soviet bases

Russians tested their first atomic bomb and Mao Tse-tung's Communists gained control of China. The discovery at about the same time of Communist spies and sympathizers within the USA itself produced an almost hysterical fear of Communism, a 'Reds under the beds' scare, among the American people culminating in the notorious McCarthy witch-hunts.

Congress can conduct investigations into any aspect of American life or government by establishing a Committee of Inquiry. One such committee in the early 1950's investigated Communism in the USA and was chaired by Senator McCarthy. Prominent people like the atomic scientist Robert Oppenheimer whom McCarthy believed to be Communists were forced to appear before the committee. Then McCarthy interrogated them like an inquisitor and

The Truman Doctrine of 1947 stated that 'it must be the policy of the United States to support free peoples who are resisting attempted subjugation by armed minorities or by outside pressures'. Later it was said that the U.S.A. must aim at 'containment of Russian expansionist tendencies'.

South Korea

Taiwan

S.E.A.T.O.

China

although often nothing could be proved against them the publicity was enough to ruin their careers.

## Containment and Cold War

By 1947 the USA had decided that the spread of Communism must be contained. To do this, it ringed the two giant Communist powers round with a series of military alliances and bases.

The Soviet Union and China, of course, viewed this encirclement as a threat to their own security. To counter NATO in the west, the USSR banded her satellite countries in Eastern Europe into the Warsaw Pact and in the east signed a defence treaty with China. Thus the greater part of the world was divided into two heavily armed camps, one dominated by the USA and the other by the Soviet Union and China. The two camps constantly menaced each other by word and action. A state only just short of open war existed between them – a cold war.

From time to time the cold war seemed likely to erupt into a hot war, as incidents occurred which threatened to involve the super-powers in direct conflict. Most of the flashpoints were located around the Sino-Soviet bloc and included most notably Berlin, Korea and Vietnam. Korea cost the

Anti-Vietnam demonstration

An American serviceman in Vietnam

USA 130,000 casualties – 'that crazy Asian war' a pop song called it. But ten years after hostilities in Korea had ceased, the USA became involved in another Asian conflict to try and check the spread of Communism.

Vietnam was to become the most hated war in American history. For a decade, like a running sore, it drained the USA of men, money and equipment. It divided the nation, wrecked the career of a President and brought the American economy dangerously close to collapse. And from the American point of view all their sacrifice was in vain. Only a year after the USA had withdrawn its last combat troops, South Vietnam fell to the Communists.

# When the world held its breath

The most dangerous flashpoint of all, however, was not in the zone of containment around the Sino-Soviet bloc but on the USA's own doorstep. In October 1962, American spy planes made the alarming discovery that the Russians had installed missile bases on the Communist-ruled island of Cuba, only 150 kilometres off the tip of Florida. Immediately, the USA threw a naval blockade around Cuba, to prevent any further supplies of Russian weapons reaching the island. For 72 hours the world held its breath, as more than a score of Soviet ships, strung out across the Atlantic, steamed slowly towards the Caribbean and the American naval force waiting to intercept them. But at the last moment the Russian ships turned back; the missile bases were later dismantled and the crisis passed away. Relations between the USA and USSR, shocked at coming so close to full scale nuclear war, actually improved. In 1963 a 'hot line' was established between Moscow and Washington and, together with Britain, the two super-powers signed a nuclear test ban treaty.

**Flashpoints**

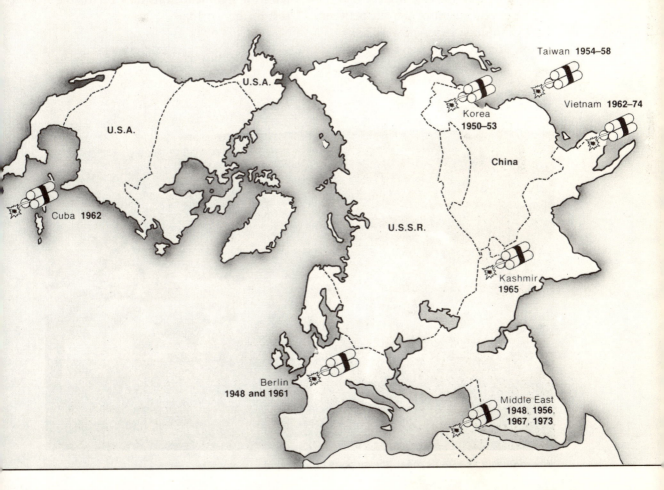

Taiwan 1954–58

Korea 1950–53

Vietnam 1962–74

China

Cuba 1962

U.S.A.

U.S.A.

U.S.S.R.

Kashmir 1965

Berlin 1948 and 1961

Middle East 1948, 1956, 1967, 1973

# Sino-Soviet split

*'Renegade clique of revisionists'*

*'New Tsars whose fascist heel tramples on the Motherland'*

*'Dogmatists'*

*'Social imperialists'*

*'Military dictatorship with great power ambitions'*

This is part of the war of words between China and the Soviet Union, which has now been going on for several years. Who do you think said what?

The development of the rift between the Communist super-powers has centred upon two key issues:

First, there is the border dispute. China has demanded the return of those parts of the old Chinese Empire which she was forced to surrender to Russia by the terms of 'unequal treaties' in the nineteenth century.

Second, there is the ideological dispute. Both China and the Soviet Union argue that their particular brand of Communism is the correct one, and therefore both claim the leadership of the Communist world.

The rift between them has now widened to such an extent that reconciliation seems very unlikely, at least in the immediate future. No one can yet tell how significant this may be for the rest of the world.

Where Russia and China meet: the steppes of Mongolia

# Spheres of influence

The super-powers regard certain parts of the world as being vital to their security. They aim to dominate such areas by maintaining a military presence in them or by making them economically subservient. Any interference by one super-power in another's sphere of influence is strongly resented and may be actively resisted, as happened in the Cuba crisis. Because each super-power exercises its most effective influence over those areas which lie immediately next to it, it has the advantage of being able to deploy its forces there more easily than any rival. When the Russians backed down over Cuba and the Americans withdrew from Vietnam, both were admitting the difficulty of sustaining a military role in places so far from home.

So, as you look at a map of the world, the super-powers may be thought of as super stars pulling smaller countries lying nearby into their fields of attraction.

Ironically, it is the two Communist giants which seem to be the most active in trying to upset this simple pattern, by promoting discord and disunity amongst each other's satellite states. Tiny Albania provides China with a toehold in the USSR's European camp, while South East Asia has been described as '*the principal diplomatic playground of the Sino-Soviet split*'.

The photographs show some examples of the various kinds of help which the super-powers give to the poor, underdeveloped countries of the Third World. Such aid is often criticized as being wholly inadequate. Even the American contribution, far greater than that of China and the USSR combined, amounts to less than 1 per cent of the total US national income. But when they dispense foreign aid, whether cash or technical advice, the super-powers are not motivated by charitable concern so much as by self-interest. They are seeking to win the friendship and secure the support of those countries not yet committed to either a capitalist or Communist way of life.

The USA hopes that the aid which it gives to backward countries will help them to modernize their economies and improve their standard of living, so reducing the risk of a Communist takeover. The Soviet Union and China hope to gain strategic footholds in Africa and Latin America, perhaps places where they can set up military

Egypt's Aswan Dam: built with Russian aid

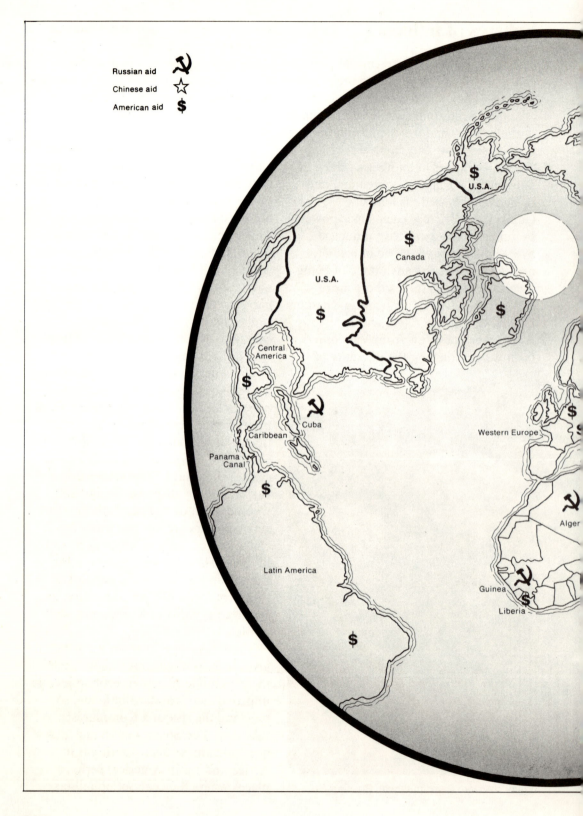

Russian aid ☭
Chinese aid ☆
American aid $

U.S.A. $

Canada $

U.S.A. $

$

Central America

☭ Cuba

$ Caribbean

Panama Canal

$

Latin America

$

Western Europe $

$

☭ Alger

☭ Guinea $

Liberia

# Spheres of influence

Pacific Ocean

Japan

Korea

Taiwan

Mongolia

China

U.S.S.R.

Philippines

S.E. Asia

Indian Ocean

Israel

Middle East

Egypt

Somalia

Sudan

Ethiopia

Kenya

East Africa

Zaire

Tanzania

Zambia

Angola

Rhodesia

South Africa

South Africa is ruled by a minority white government. Rhodesia (Zimbabwe) was ruled by a white minority government until 1978.

Chinese aid in Africa: Tanzanian children wave at one of the first trains (above) along the Chinese – financed and constructed Tanzam railway (below) connecting Zambia to the sea through Tanzania

bases. As already noted, the Chinese see their own revolutionary model as being particularly suitable for export to the Third World. What do you think they mean when they talk about '*people's wars sweeping over the world countryside and eventually encircling the cities of the world*'?

The most dangerous flashpoint in the world today is almost certainly the Middle East. Both the USA and USSR have vital interests in this region, which contains two thirds of the world's known oil reserves and provides a gateway from the Mediterranean to the Indian Ocean. In the past the Americans have supported the Israelis, and the Russians have backed the Arabs, in the frequent wars which have flared up between the two groups. Recently, however, the super-powers seem to have been working together to try and bring peace and stability to this troubled area. Here perhaps is evidence of a new spirit of co-operation growing up between the USA and USSR replacing the hostility of the cold war.

# The Space Race

| | USA | USSR | China |
|---|---|---|---|
| 1957 | | **Sputnik 1**, the first artificial satellite, is launched | |
| 1959 | | **Lunik 3** photographs far side of moon | |
| 1961 | | **Yuri Gagarin** is first man to orbit the earth | |
| 1962 | **John Glenn** orbits earth | | |
| 1963 | | **Valentina Tereschova** is first woman in space | |
| 1964 | | **Voshkod**, the first three-man satellite, is launched | |
| 1968 | **Apollo 8** orbits the moon | | |
| 1969 | **Apollo 11** lands on the moon. **Neil Armstrong** and **Edward Aldrin** are first men to walk on surface of moon | | |
| 1970 | | | First satellite launched |
| 1972 | **Apollo 16** explores mountains of moon | | |
| 1975 | **Apollo–Soyuz** mission | | |

The crews and craft of the joint Soyuz-Apollo space flight, 1975

# A handshake in space

In July 1975, a joint Soviet–US space project culminated in the docking of Soyuz and Apollo spacecraft and a handshake in space. This remarkable picture was beamed down from space to millions of television viewers around the earth. It symbolized perhaps the closing of one chapter and the opening of another. In space more than in any other field during the preceding two decades, the rivalry between the USA and USSR had been spotlighted for all the world to watch. Spurred on by concern for national security and desire for national prestige, the two super-powers poured vast sums of money into their space programmes, money which critics said would have been better spent improving life on earth. A spectacular success by one power would quickly be matched or outdone by the other.

The greatest technological feat of all must be the Apollo moon landings. *'One small step for a man, one giant leap for mankind'*, said Neil Armstrong in 1969, as he became the first man to step on to the surface of the moon. Yet the most significant mission of all may yet prove to be the joint Soyuz-Apollo flight in July 1975. The handshake between the Russian cosmonauts and the American astronauts high over the divided continent of Europe may be seen in retrospect to have ushered in a new era of co-operation between the super-powers.

## From deterrent to détente

After the Cuba crisis, the USA and USSR gradually began to adopt a less aggressive attitude towards each other. While both continued to stress the superiority and desirability of their own political and economic systems, they also said that it was possible for them to co-exist peacefully in the world.

For some time the Chinese refused to accept this policy, but increasing contact took place between them and the Americans in the early 1970's, during which time China was admitted to the United Nations and President Nixon visited Peking. The American president

Neil Armstrong plants the US flag on the Moon

indeed referred to his visit as '*the week that changed the world*'. No doubt this was an exaggeration but at least tension between China and the USA was reduced.

At the same time relations between the USA and USSR were further eased when the leaders of the two countries visited each other's capitals and signed trade agreements. This and the Helsinki security conference in 1975 seemed to indicate that these two super-powers were beginning to move from a policy of mere co-existence to one of active

Nixon and Mao in Conference

co-operation. This policy is called détente.

**'*We shall bury you*',**

a Russian leader warned the Americans at the height of the cold war. How seriously this threat was intended to be taken is open to debate, but certainly it has often been said that if the '*East and West don't bury their differences they will bury each other*'. As the only alternative to a nuclear holocaust, therefore, everyone would agree that genuine détente is to be welcomed.

But some western spokesmen argue that détente like Munich '*feeds and encourages the forces of war and totalitarianism*'. They point with alarm at the Soviet Union's massive military budget, at the expansion of her navy and her increasing activity in the Indian Ocean. Is this evidence of a real desire for peace they ask? Is détente merely a mask lulling the West into a false sense of security? The supporters of détente claim that it '*offers the only detour, the only accessible turn-off, from the collision course of the super-powers*'.

What is your view? Is détente the answer, or '*a policy of firm resistance to Communist expansion backed by the military means to make the policy credible*'? Which is the best way to keep peace and prevent World War III, a war which would open and not close with the use of nuclear weapons?

The opening of the SALT talks on arms limitation, Vienna, April 1970.

## Further reading and reference

*A Map History of the Modern World*
B Catchpole · Heinemann

*Wars of the Twentieth Century*
S L Mayer · Octopus

*A History of the People's Democracies*
F Fejitö · Penguin

*Soviet Foreign Policy 1962–1973*
R Edmonds · OUP

*The Best and the Brightest*
D Halberstam · Pan

*An Eye for the Dragon*
D Bloodworth · Penguin

*The Nuclear Trap*
R E Walters · Penguin

## Discussion

**1** *'Appeasement by another name.'*
Do you think that this is a fair view of détente?

**2** *'The USA has taken over from Britain the rôle of the world's policeman.'*
How well do you consider that this describes the part played by the USA in world affairs since the end of World War II?

**3** *'Better Red than dead.'*
Do you agree?

**4** *'Charity begins at home.'*
Do you think that the super-powers and Britain should:
**a** do more to improve conditions at home before sending aid abroad?

**b** insist that underdeveloped countries do more to help themselves?

**5** *'A waste of time and money.'*
What is your view of the space programmes mounted by the super-powers?

**6** *'Twisting the lion's tail has become a favourite occupation amongst some of the world's smaller countries.'*
**a** What evidence can you find to support this assertion with reference to Britain?
**b** How far do you think that the same assertion is true with reference to the super-powers?

**7** *'We shall pay any price, bear any burden, meet any hardship, oppose any foe, to assure the survival and the success of liberty.'*
How far do you think that these promises made by John F Kennedy in 1961 have been fulfilled in American foreign policy?

## Analysis

**1** In 1949 the Russians blockaded West Berlin and refused to allow the Allies (USA, Britain and France) to bring in supplies by land.
**a** How were the Allies able to overcome the Berlin blockade?
**b** What do you think is meant by the claim that the *'Allies won the war in Europe but lost the peace.'*?
**c** In what sense are the countries of Eastern Europe satellites of the Soviet Union? What events occurred in Eastern Europe in 1956 and 1968?

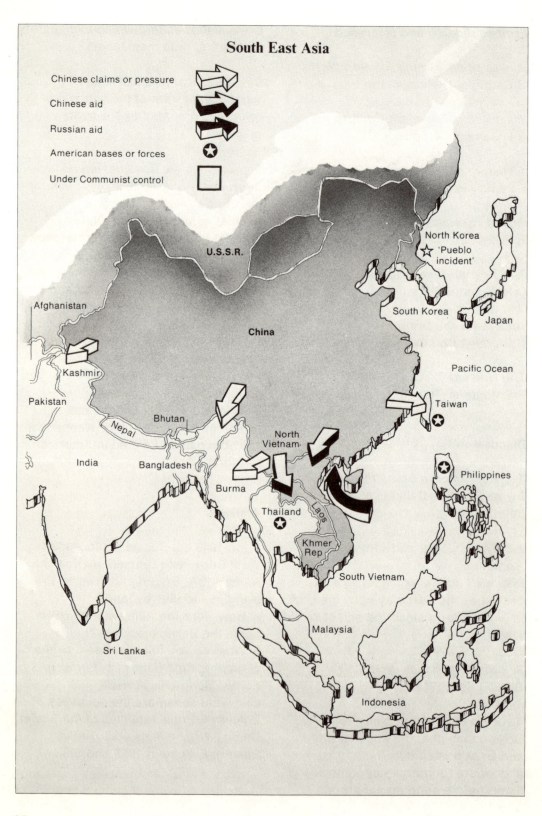

# South East Asia

Chinese claims or pressure

Chinese aid

Russian aid

American bases or forces

Under Communist control

U.S.S.R.

North Korea
'Pueblo incident'

South Korea

Japan

Afghanistan

China

Pacific Ocean

Kashmir

Taiwan

Pakistan

Nepal

Bhutan

North Vietnam

India

Bangladesh

Burma

Philippines

Thailand

Laos

Khmer Rep

South Vietnam

Malaysia

Sri Lanka

Indonesia

**2** The Korean War lasted from 1950 to 1953.

Taiwan is perhaps the main stumbling block to the normalization of relations between China and the USA.

## Korea and Taiwan

**1910–45**
Korea a Japanese colony

**1945**
Russians invade North Korea. Americans invade South Korea. Dividing line is 38th Parallel

**1948**
Russians withdraw leaving North Korea as a Communist state

**1949**
Americans withdraw leaving South Korea as a democratic state. Communists gain control of China. Nationalist forces flee to Taiwan

**1950**
North Korea invades South Korea. UN forces, mainly American, drive North Koreans back. Chinese forces intervene to help North Korea

**1953**
Armistice in Korea

**1954**
USA signs defence treaty with Taiwan

**1968**
'Pueblo' incident

**1971**
Taiwan expelled from United Nations. Communist China admitted

**a** What was the cause of the Korean War?
**b** How did the Americans and Chinese become involved in the Korean War and what part did they play?
**c** What was the Pueblo incident?
**d** What is the nature of the Chinese claim and the American commitment to Taiwan?

**3** Originally SE Asia was French Indo-China. For many years first the French and then the Americans fought local Communist guerrillas in the region. The Communist forces were supported by the Soviet Union and China, which are competing to establish overall influence in the area.
**a** How was North Vietnam established as a sovereign state?
**b** How did the USA get involved in the Vietnam war?
**c** Why did the Vietnam war prove:
– so difficult for the Americans to fight?
– so unpopular with the American people?
**d** What is the 'domino theory'? How far has it been borne out? In what ways could SE Asia be considered to be of strategic value to the USA?

**4** The following map shows the balance of forces between NATO and the Warsaw Pact countries:
**a** Apart from their superiority in numbers what other advantages do the Warsaw Pact forces have over those of NATO?
**b** *'It is extremely risky for Britain to shelter under America's nuclear umbrella'*
– How would you interpret this statement?
– What American bases are there in Britain? Do you think that Britain

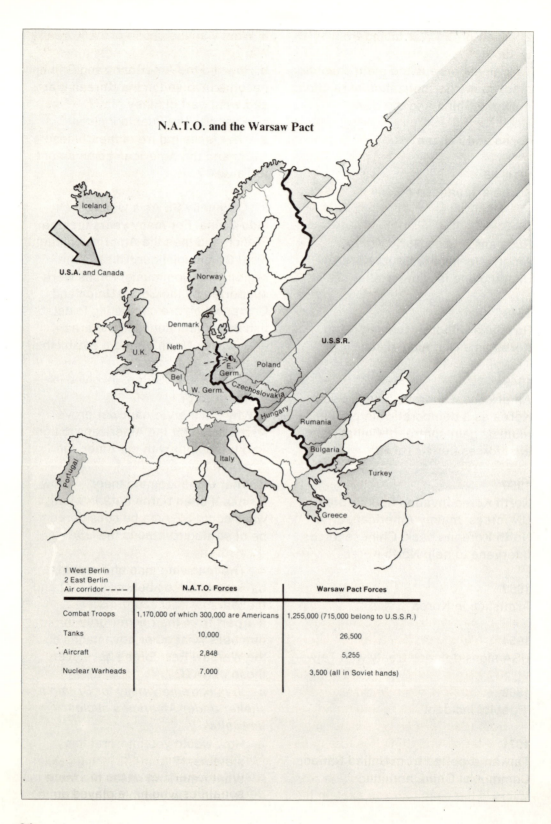

## N.A.T.O. and the Warsaw Pact

Iceland

U.S.A. and Canada

Norway

Denmark

Neth

U.K.

Bel

W. Germ.

E. Germ.

Poland

U.S.S.R.

Czechoslovakia

Hungary

Rumania

Bulgaria

Italy

Portugal

Turkey

Greece

1 West Berlin
2 East Berlin
Air corridor – – – –

| | N.A.T.O. Forces | Warsaw Pact Forces |
|---|---|---|
| Combat Troops | 1,170,000 of which 300,000 are Americans | 1,255,000 (715,000 belong to U.S.S.R.) |
| Tanks | 10,000 | 26,500 |
| Aircraft | 2,848 | 5,255 |
| Nuclear Warheads | 7,000 | 3,500 (all in Soviet hands) |

should continue to provide the USA with these facilities?
- Do you think that Britain should maintain an independent nuclear deterrent?

c Why were the south eastern and south western flanks of NATO causing the USA some concern in 1974–75?

5 The following lists show the main recipients of post-war aid from the USA and the USSR (in descending order, according to the amount received):

| USA | USSR |
| --- | --- |
| United Kingdom | Mongolia |
| India | China |
| France | Bulgaria |
| South Vietnam | North Vietnam |
| Pakistan | Poland |
| Italy | Cuba |
| Japan | Rumania |
| Taiwan | Egypt |
| Yugoslavia | Hungary |
| Brazil | Algeria |
| Turkey | Afghanistan |
| Greece | North Korea |
| Philippines | Iraq |
| Egypt | India |
| Austria | Iran |
| | Philippines |

a Map the countries receiving aid.
b Which of these countries do you consider most likely:
- to have received most of their aid immediately after World War II?
- to be cut off from receiving any aid from their former benefactor now?
c How far do you think it is true to say that most of the recipients of Soviet aid are small and strategically located? If this is the case can you explain it?

d How many recipients of American aid are in the zone of containment?
e Which two continental areas have received little aid from either super-power?

6 The following newspaper item indicates one aspect of the three-cornered contest between the super-powers to gain influence in Africa.

New Soviet arms shipments to the pro-Moscow faction in Angola and America's first arms deal with the Kenyan Government underline the competition that goes on in Africa despite talk of détente elsewhere.

a What is the present situation in Angola?
b Have events borne out the view held by the USSR and China that:
'*Africa must naturally be ripe for communist revolution*'?
What considerations do you think such a view has been based on?
c What circumstances make it particularly difficult for the super-powers to establish any permanent influence in Africa?
d '*If the Middle East is pacified the next major international trouble-spot could be East Africa.*'
What grounds are there for making such a prophecy?

**Seminars**

For tutorial seminars produce biographical sketches of the following personalities who have played an important part in shaping or influencing the foreign policies of the super-powers in the last twenty-five years:

Eisenhower — Nixon
Kruschev — Brezhnev
Dulles — Kissinger
J F Kennedy — Ho Chi Minh
Johnson — Castro

**Investigation**

1   What are the main features which characterize the following:

a  Iron Curtain
b  Hot Line?

2   What was the significance of:

a  Munich 1938
b  Marshall Aid
c  Monroe Doctrine
d  Truman Doctrine?

3   What is the Security Council of the United Nations? What position do the super-powers hold on it?

# Acknowledgements

Acknowledgements are due to the following for permission to reproduce photographs in this book:

Camera Press Ltd: 5, 8, 11, 14 (left), 21, 22 (top), 24, 25, 31 (top), 37 (top), 47, 50 (top and bottom), 54, 61, 74 (top and bottom), 79, 80, 82, 83, 86 (top and bottom);   Associated Press Ltd: 6–7, 25;   Popperfoto: 6–7, 34;   Keystone Press Agency Ltd: 14 (right), 20, 23, 36 (bottom), 40 (bottom), 57, 73, 89 (top), 90;   Richard and Sally Greenhill: 15 (top);   Radio Times Hulton Picture Library: 15 (bottom), 26;   The Mansell Collection: 17, 28–9;   John Hillelson Agency Ltd/Chuck Isaacs/Magnum: 22 (bottom);   Mary Evans Picture Library: 27, 40 (top);   John Hillelson Agency Ltd/Marc Riboud/Magnum: 31 (bottom), 32;   Novosti Press Agency: 43, 46, 51, 52, 88 (top and bottom):   John Hillelson Agency Ltd/ Georg Gerster: 56, 66;   John Hillelson Agency Ltd/ James Mitchell/Magnum: 68;   United States Information Service: 89 (bottom).